# Thank God it's Monday

## Ministry in the workplace

**Mark Greene**

Scripture Union, 207-209 Queensway, Bletchley, MK2 2EB, England.

First published 1994, reprinted 1995
Second edition 1997, reprinted 1998, 1999

ISBN 1 85999 208 0, 2nd edition
(ISBN 0 86201 908 7, 1st edition)

British Library Cataloguing-in-Publication Data
A catalogue record for this book is available from the British Library.

Cover design by ie Design.
Cover illustration by Chris Lloyd.

Printed and bound in Great Britain by Cox & Wyman Ltd, Reading, Berkshire.

*This book is dedicated with love and gratitude
to the memory of Robert Martel (1958–1994)
secretary, colleague, example, friend
who knew the secret
(Philippians 4:11–12)*

# CONTENTS

| | First thoughts | 7 |
|---|---|---|
| | Second thoughts | 8 |
| 1 | Into the lion's den | 11 |
| 2 | Another day, another dime? | 29 |
| 3 | Winning away | 41 |
| 4 | The camomile factor | 47 |
| 5 | Edge without guilt | 61 |
| 6 | Getting going | 79 |
| 7 | The body business | 85 |
| 8 | Romeo/Juliet | 93 |
| 9 | Work is a seven-letter word | 99 |
| 10 | Who's the king of the castle? | 109 |
| 11 | Rebel, rebel | 131 |
| 12 | Life on the crash barrier | 137 |
| 13 | Lies "R" Us | 147 |
| 14 | When the heat is on | 165 |
| 15 | You're the boss too? | 175 |

## ACKNOWLEDGMENTS

Thanks particularly to:

My colleagues at Ogilvy & Mather, who put up with me

The people of Trinity Baptist Church, New York, who gave me so much

Bill Vallari and Jill Vellinger – examples and encouragers at work

Glen Kleinknecht, who first suggested that I write this book

Alison Barr, my editor, who made it better

Dr Peter Cotterell, who vetted it for error of all kinds

The students of London Bible College (probably the finest theological college in the world and certainly the best one in Northwood), who prayed for me to get it finished

Katriina Greene, a minister in her workplace and my wife, who made it possible for me to get it finished

• • •

# First thoughts

## (Spring 1994)

There are a lot of stories in this book.

They are all true.

Some of them are about success. Some of them are about abject failure. They are all about God at work. Indeed, there were days when God seemed to be doing so many things that I hardly had time to record them all in my diary. Amazing, exhilarating times they were.

As I look back on all that happened, what hits me again and again is a sense of wonder – our God cares, our God is at work, our God uses us, with all our clumsiness and mixed motives and lack of knowledge. Our God does great things.

I have told these stories not to suggest that God will act in the same way in your workplace – may he move in even greater ways – but simply to illustrate that he is at work – at work. That the God who brought water from the rock, who changed water into wine, who raised Lazarus from the dead, does great things today. Indeed, as I look back I am filled with wonder at his power, timing, sense of humour, grace and ability to use even the most unpromising circumstances for his ends. It was a joyous privilege to experience this. I wish you that joy.

• • •

# Second thoughts

## (Summer 1997)

It's 9.02.

Jim has been at work for an hour and a half.

He is young and has been working for this City firm for less than two years.

His boss calls him into his office. He tells Jim he's fired and he has until lunchtime to clear his desk.

A woman is standing next to a bus stop, and gets talking to an eleven-year-old boy.

'What do you want to be when you grow up?' she asks.

'Employed,' he replies.

David has just graduated with honours in Computer Science. He has found a job. He has a six-month contract. He is very grateful.

The expectations and conditions of work have changed massively in the last ten years. People – even those employed in what used to be the secure world of banking – don't expect to be with the same company in five years' or even three years' time. They have lived with the threat and the reality of redundancy, and the threat and reality of long-term unemployment. They have seen companies shrink and the proportion of freelance, casual and part-time workers rise. They recognise that whatever employer/employee loyalty used to mean, it now means something different.

It is a time of anxiety, not just stress. A time when the balance of power seems to have shifted markedly in favour of employers over employees. A time when shareholders call the shots. A time when British white-collar workers work for longer hours than their European counterparts, but not necessarily for higher wages. A time when we have the growing absurdity of a system in which if you are working you are likely to be overworked, but if you are not you are likely to have more time on your hands than you know what to do with. A time when you can work forty hours a week for a reputable company, but not make a living wage. A time when honesty is on the wane, and interest in business ethics is on the rise.

For such a changing time as this, with all its uncertainties, God's people are still called to shine like stars.

It is getting tougher, and I have revised this book to reflect the new conditions at work today. However, despite the problems, week by week I meet more and more men and women who are consciously committed to seeing the contemporary workplace transformed. Men and women who have seen God work in extraordinary ways in their lives and in the lives of their co-workers. Men and women who know that he has gone with them into their Jerusalems, Judeas and Samarias, even to the ends of the earth. That he has done great things, and will continue to do so.

*Mark Greene*

# • 1 •

# INTO THE LION'S DEN

### or
### The 'No go' zone

*'Surely the Lord is in this place,*
*and I was not aware of it.'*

Genesis 28:16

## • SNAPSHOTS •

I am a Jewish Christian and it is the second night of Passover. A group of us are going to celebrate it together in my flat. One of the people coming has prepared a chicken. She brings it to work, and we decide to put it in the fridge in my boss's office. My boss is out that week. But David Ogilvy – the man who founded the company I work for, and the world's greatest living adman – is visiting and using the office, off and on.

. I have wanted to talk to him about God. I have prayed for an opportunity to talk to him about God. But so far I haven't found either the courage or the opportunity. Or the courage to try to create the opportunity. I am very junior, and he is the founder of the world's fourth largest advertising agency.

At four o'clock that afternoon, I realise it is time to collect the chicken and go and prepare the Passover. I wander round to my boss's office. David Ogilvy is in there talking on the phone. I wait a couple of minutes. The talking stops.

He is in there. And he has my chicken.

I'm out here. And I have six people coming for supper. It's getting late.

How should I introduce myself to the founder of the fourth largest advertising agency in the world? Will I be fired for trying to convert the founder? What should I say to the world's greatest living adman? Perhaps 'Hello, I've come to collect my chicken'?

I realise that God is using this dead, half-roasted chicken to force me into David Ogilvy's presence. And I am sure that God who knows both my lack of courage and my taste for bad puns has had a lot of fun choosing a 'chicken' as the thing that forces me to overcome my cowardice.

I knock. I walk into the lion's den. All my clever lines desert me. The greatest living adman looks up and says, 'Come in, sit down, who are you?' We talk for an hour or so – and somehow the conversation turns quickly and easily to God.

God at work.

And I wasn't fired.

We're in a bar having a farewell drink for one of the team. I'm talking to Susan. We have been working together for about a year, and we get round to C S Lewis. Barbara (or at least that's what we'll call her) is with us. She's Jewish, bright and fun.

'Is that the same C S Lewis who wrote the Narnia Chronicles?'

'Yes.'

'I love those books. He's my hero. I didn't know he was a Christian.'

'Oh yes, and there's Christian allegory in the books. Aslan is Jesus…'

'Yeah, but Aslan comes back to life...'
God at work. The Christian at work.

It's two o'clock in the afternoon.
He is not having a very wonderful day.
An angel comes and leaves a chocolate on his desk.
The Christian at work.

Three aspects of ministry in the workplace.

David Ogilvy – the opportunities God gives us when we step outside our circle of confidence.

Barbara and C S Lewis – the opportunities God gives us when we spend time with people outside the workplace.

A chocolate on the desk – the opportunities God gives us to express love and kindness to those we work with in our everyday routine.

The workplace is God's place, and his place is just as much there as in the church prayer-meeting. The workplace is a place of opportunity – a place to express the compassion of the gospel in word and deed, to challenge non-biblical thinking and practice, to grow in faith and character and love.

God at work in us.
God at work through us.
God at work in those we work with.

• • •

## GOD'S PLACE

There are few subjects I feel are more neglected, few issues that excite me more, few areas of ministry that could do more to transform the nature of society than witness at work. There are few things that could do more to invigorate and release us as Christians than to be equipped for ministry in the place where many of us spend sixty to seventy percent of our waking lives...

It is putting workplace ministry on the agenda that I am most concerned about. I am concerned about it because I am concerned about people – that all may be saved. And I am concerned about society – that the meat may be salted and the rot stopped.

The church today is engaged in a Decade of Evangelism. The church is doing its research and concluding that the people on the fringes of today's churches are fewer and fewer. That the people who know even the basics of Christian claims are fewer and fewer. That the church must go out to the people on the fringe and the people beyond the fringe, and win them there. That the church must develop services for them that are in their language, not ours.

Indeed. But where, in all this grand strategy, have we heard anyone whisper, 'The workplace'?

We are encouraged to develop relationships with our neighbours. Quite right. We are encouraged to develop relationships with non-Christian friends. Quite right. But how much time do you spend with even your best friend in a month? Two hours, three hours, four hours? Ten hours?

We are encouraged to bring people to guest services. We are encouraged to sing carols outside Tesco or to get involved in putting on a concert to which we will invite our non-Christian friends. All good things. But are we encouraged to witness at work?

The overwhelming answer in most cases is 'No' – 75% of the people I have surveyed have never been asked by their minister about their ministry in their workplace.

## PEANUTS AND PUDDLES

Are we working at the margins and forgetting the centre? Playing with peanuts and aperitifs when there is a main course to get stuck into? Sending Christians out into the highways and byways when the room is full of people? Struggling to develop relationships with the strangers next door when our neighbour is just a desk away?

This is a great tragedy. Because Christians in work spend more time in the workplace than in any other place. The workplace is, day in, day out, the one place where non-Christians can see the difference that being a Christian makes – the one place where Christian and non-Christian face the same stresses, may have the same boss, may be rebuked for similar failures, praised for similar successes, are subject to the same structural dynamics, to the same corporate culture, the same food, the same gossip...

There are very few places where a non-Christian could and should see the difference that Christ makes in a life so clearly as in working with someone thirty, forty, sixty hours a week.

We are being called on to look for common ground with non-Christians when, *in the workplace*, we already share it.

We are being exhorted to build bridges when, *in the workplace*, the bridges are already built and have been crossed.

We are exhorted to go and develop relationships with people but, *in the workplace*, the relationships already exist.

We are encouraged to go out and fish in pools and puddles when we are sitting on a lake full of fish.

## THE UNAVOIDABLE WITNESS

Importantly, in the workplace the witness comes in a form that cannot be tuned out like a radio programme, zapped like a television broadcast, thrown away like a tract or turned down like the invitation to a concert.

The non-Christian can tune out almost every form of the gospel, but he cannot – short of murder or machiavellian office politics – tune out the spectacle of the Christian living in the power of the Spirit day by day, hour by hour, crisis by crisis.

Furthermore, the workplace is the one place where Christians can't avoid contact with non-Christians. In every other area we can schedule non-Christians out – making friends mainly with Christians, ministering in a housegroup, serving on a church committee, going to the church prayer-meeting, attending church on Sunday. And so on. The workplace is the one place where Christians are forced to meet non-Christians. The one place where Christian and non-Christian have to relate to one another. That's why it is critical for evangelism.

If the church is looking for people who are beyond the fringe, it will find many of them in the same workplaces as their members. If the church is looking to stop the rot, it will find that the rot is in many of the companies for which its members work – where there are poor payment practices, the abuse of smaller suppliers, unjust appraisal systems, racist or sexist hiring policies, bribery, corruption, dirty tricks campaigns, competitiveness which is not a spur to excellence but a goad to deceit. As John Stott put it, you can't blame the meat for going rotten, blame the salt...

But for most Christians work is not a mission field. Work is not a primary or even a secondary context for ministry. And work is not the place to challenge non-Christian worldviews and management practices.

Why not?

## PRESSURE FROM SOCIETY?

Society encourages us to believe that our faith is private and has no place in the working world. Indeed, the working world operates on an atheistic basis. God, it believes, does not show up on the balance sheet. What we do in our own time is up to us, but there is no place for biblical ethics and claims about truth on the factory floor or in the board meeting.

This anti-Christian prejudice leads to fear of not fitting in, fear of not getting promoted, fear of losing my job. If I do speak out for my faith, if I refuse to tap into a rival airline's computers – will I still be getting a paycheque next month? Real fears, with plenty of foundation in experience.

## THE CHURCH AGAINST EVANGELISM?

However, in many cases the major source of pressure against witness at work comes from the local church. Most churches are in fact, if not by conviction, primarily focused on building up their own local congregation.

The minister's concerns relate to his neighbourhood, and he rightly wants his church community to be engaged in evangelism. As a result, the church develops programmes that relate to the concerns of people in the immediate area. In turn, the minister mobilises resources behind this neighbourhood effort.

However, for the most part, church programmes encourage us to relate to cold contacts – people we don't know that well, people we haven't met until we stand outside Tesco or knock on their doors, people who are our neighbours but who often only want a semi-detached kind of relationship with those living close by. Church evangelism is, if you like, a cold contact farm.

Today, however, many people's primary relationships are not in their neighbourhood. Changes in work and transport patterns mean that the people we spend most time with often don't live near the church.

Many of our warm contacts are at work.

If we are looking for contacts, then this may well be the place to begin. After all, the average person probably meets, talks to, eats with, writes to, works with over a hundred people a week.

Warm contacts.

## THE FORGOTTEN KINGDOM

The local church, therefore, may well be mobilised to 'do church' in a particular neighbourhood, rather than equip its people to build the kingdom wherever God has placed them. And this may be further reflected in the way church members are encouraged.

If you go to the deacons' meeting you are affirmed by your fellow Christians, by the leadership of the church. If you stay on at the office to go out for a drink with a co-worker you are not. In other words, there is no mechanism for affirmation of the working person – except in crisis. Indeed, 50% of the Christians I have surveyed have never heard a single sermon on work. That is, they have never had any biblical teaching on the area of life that is meant to occupy them six days a week.

For what ministry, then, are our ministers equipping their flocks? Probably for the ministries of the local church. For the ministries that revolve around the minister's skills and gifts. In other words, are our leaders inadvertently equipping us to support *their* ministry rather than equipping us to do the work of *ours*?

Is your minister looking to see how your gifts can fit into the church's needs? Or is he asking how God can use you to further the work of the kingdom? Is he asking where else, apart from in this church, has God placed you? To what ministry are you called? Where is God calling you to exercise your gifts? If my research is anything to go by, I suspect not.

There is a significant danger that church evangelistic strategies will inadvertently be designed around getting people into church to hear the minister, when the more important issue is getting people into the kingdom by hearing the word of God. Of course, our leaders are not deliberately seeking to inhibit our ministry or to build their own. Work has simply become unimportant on all our spiritual agendas.

If you are a good Bible study leader, do you think to yourself, 'I'd like to take on a housegroup'? Or do you think, 'You know, I'm quite good at leading Bible studies. Maybe I should start one at work'? And it's a rare thing indeed for someone to come up and ask you, 'How's your witness at work? What particular issues are you facing there?'

This is also reflected in preaching and teaching. As I've mentioned, over 50% of Christians I have surveyed have never heard a sermon on work. Over 70% have never been taught a theology of work. Which is even more extraordinary when you think that most people who have been Christians for more than three years have probably heard sermons on Genesis 1–3, which, as we will see later, is no bad place to start looking for a theology of work. Seventy-five percent have never been taught a theology of vocation. Under 25% have ever been asked by their minister about their witness at work. Whereas I suspect that almost everyone who has been in a church for more than a year has been encouraged to get involved with one of the church's ministries. Finally, only 26% have ever been asked by their minister to consider developing a ministry in the workplace.

Sobering statistics. The reality of the overall situation is probably far worse since this research was conducted among highly motivated groups.

## AN UNHOLY HIERARCHY

This overall marginalisation of work is further reflected in a belief within the church which goes something like this:

> All Christians are born equal, but 'full-time'
> Christians are more equal than others.

In turn, there is an unspoken hierarchy that goes something like this:

Pastor
Overseas missionary
Full-time Christian worker
Tentmaker (as long as it's abroad)
Elder
Deacon
Poor Christian
Christian
Rich Christian
Former advertising executives

The fact is that we have, to a very large extent, completely lost the sense that God might call someone to a secular job or indeed to unpaid work in the home, and that either of these may be just as strategic in his economy as pastoring a church. We no longer have a theology of vocation.

Indeed, it is very easy for students training in theological institutions to be apologetic or defensive if they feel God is calling them into secular work. As if it were second best. Others may feel pressured into going into full-time Christian work by the expectations of their church and supporters: 'We haven't sent you to Bible College for three years just so you can go back into the oil business'. And that, I believe, reveals our lack of belief in 2 Timothy 3:16–17:

All Scripture is God-breathed and is useful for
teaching, rebuking, correcting and training in righteousness, so that the man of God may be thor-
oughly equipped for every good work.

For *every* good work. But when someone leaves school
or university or Bible College and takes a job at
Sainsbury's, will the church pray specifically for the
ministry to which God has set them apart?

It is indeed fine to study the Bible in order to use our
secular jobs as a platform for evangelism and ministry
in Saudi Arabia. But at Kodak in Harrow? The irony is
that Kodak may be an unreached people-group every
bit as needy as the Saudis. Or the Rendile in Kenya. Or
the Kalahari bushpeople. Indeed, when I started my last
secular job I was, as far as I knew, the only Christian in
that workplace. One in a thousand – 0.1% of the population. A missionary need to rival that of Tunisia, Iran
and Turkey. And, it might be added, a missionary enter-
prise that would need no funds from the church but
would be funded entirely by my employers.

In fact, one might argue that Christians need a good
theological education even more to work in a secular
organisation than to work in a church. Precisely
because the worldview of the secular organisation may
be so fundamentally opposed to Christianity, the daily
challenge of working through the variety of issues and
problems may take a great deal of discernment.
Particularly since you may well be the only Christian in
that company.

Think for a moment of the difficult ethical decisions
involved in any job in health care. Ask a Christian
teacher or lawyer about the challenges they face. Talk
to someone on the factory floor about communicating
the gospel to their workmates. Writing a sermon is
comparatively safe. At least there's a whole host of

people to tell you when you get it wrong.

So, in my view the church doesn't believe 2 Timothy 3:16–17, or there would be a flood of young people aged 18–23 spending a year or two at Bible Colleges before or after going to college or starting work. And there aren't many.

And there would be a number of Bible Colleges offering courses and options specifically designed for people going into secular work. And there aren't many.

## BELIEVE IT OR NOT?

There are several things we don't really believe:

- All vocations are equal, and so-called 'secular' work is a vocation.

- Many of our biblical heroes were, in fact, workers.

The Israelite midwives who, struggling for biblical medical ethics, boldly defied Pharaoh's command to kill all male Hebrew babies (Exod 1:15–22); Naaman's strategically placed servant girl, who courageously told her pagan master that healing was to be found in a foreign land (2 Kings 5:1–3); Lydia, the merchant (Acts 16:14–15); Joseph, the chancellor (Gen 41:41); Daniel, the imperial advisor (Dan 2:48); Nehemiah, the security agent (Neh 4:12–15). People like these are often perceived and presented as 'spiritual giants', children's heroes rather than as ordinary women and men working out their faith in their workplaces.

Here are some other things we don't really believe:

- All work needs to be done in line with the word of God and to his glory.

- God is interested in every part of our lives.

- Secular work can be a privilege and a joy.

- Proverbs is an important book of the Bible. If we believed that, there would be a lot more teaching from Proverbs. And then we would hear a lot more about work.

In sum, there is a great danger that we as Christians will accept the division non-believers make between the public world of work and the private world of faith. That we will seek to limit God's activities to non-working hours.

But does God save people in the workplace? Yes.

Does God heal in the workplace? Well, yes, in my experience he does.

Does God love justice and mercy in the workplace? Of course.

Is God's work limited in any significant way by the demands and disciplines of the workplace?

Surely not.

## THE GUILT-EDGED CHRISTIAN

The impact on Christians of effectively robbing their work of spiritual and ministry value is to produce a sense of guilt. The working Christian comes home at the end of a fifty-hour week and thinks, 'I haven't done any evangelism. I haven't done any ministry. I'm not serving God. I must make time outside work to do all these things otherwise I'm not leading an obedient Christian life.' So perhaps he or she gets involved in neighbourhood evangelism, or accepts the invitation to serve on the diaconate, and tries to squeeze a hundred commitments into a seven-day week.

The result can simply be exhaustion and discouragement. Exhaustion because too much is being attempted; discouragement because there may not be much to show for a lot of extra effort. And because there is this sneaking suspicion that the thing we spend thirty, forty, fifty hours a week doing is of no intrinsic value to God – whether it is typing letters, looking after children, fixing cars or fixing people. God isn't interested in that. After all, my minister isn't and my Christian friends aren't, so surely it follows that *he* isn't.

This unspoken but real belief stems not only from lack of encouragement but also from the failure to apply biblical truths about identity, about God's love, about the ministry of the Spirit to our working lives.

## THE ABSENTEE SPIRIT?

God doesn't change when we walk into work. But maybe *we* do.

The Holy Spirit doesn't suddenly realise he's in an office or a factory and say, 'I'm off now. See you later at the prayer meeting.'

The Holy Spirit, the Spirit of mission, doesn't say, 'Well, here we are in the office. Forget the evangelism bit, forget the gifts bit – I'm just into the fruits bit now. Let's concentrate on Galatians 5 – on love, joy, peace, patience, kindness, goodness, faithfulness, gentleness and self-control – from eight to six, and we'll get back to drawing people into relationship with Christ later on this evening.'

This book is about living an integrated Christian life at work as well as outside work. About God at work *in* our workplace as well as outside it. About living in the confidence of God's resources at work as well as outside work. About the fact that God's place is always first wherever we are, whatever we do, whoever we work for.

Of course, we can't all do all things. God doesn't call all working Christians to focus their ministry in the workplace. But I do long to see Christians released into ministry where they are.

I long to see Christians go out expectantly to work and come home exhilarated – like Jesus at the well, so empowered and thrilled by his ministry to the Samaritan woman that, though his disciples urged him to eat something, he said:

> 'I have food to eat that you know nothing about … My food … is to do the will of him who sent me and to finish his work. Do you not say, "Four months more and then the harvest"? I tell you, open your eyes and look at the fields! They are ripe for harvest.'
>
> John 4:32–35

For many, many Christians the workplace is, I believe, a harvest field. This book is about working there.

• • •

# • EPILOGUE •
## Models for our time

### On the buses
### or
### A working heroine is something to be

Penny has been on the buses for seven years.

She's a warm, down-to-earth, no-nonsense sort of lady. It's not an easy job: trying to soothe stroppy, frozen-footed, frustrated passengers who have waited forty-five minutes in the rain for the one that didn't come; trying to treat everyone who asks for a ticket as a human being, as somebody in God's plan; trying to go by the rules and not let the pensioners onto the bus before nine just because 'all the other drivers do'; trying to chat to her regulars, some of whom are just plain lonely and come out for a ride into town for the company. Trying and sometimes blowing it.

Being herself and, as she puts it, trusting that through it all God will use her somehow.

It's a tough place to work.

Lots of affairs, lots of divorce, lots of gossip. 'Pen', as they call her, tries not to get involved. Sometimes she says, 'I don't want to hear about it.' Sometimes she simply withdraws from the scene. People miss her. She responds, 'I don't want to spend my free time cooped up in an office talking about everyone's ins and outs.'

But when the chips are down it's often Pen people tell things to. After all, they can be sure she's not going to sit in an office blabbing it to the world. Similarly, it's often others who ask her questions about Jesus. They just come to her. She laughs with a mixture of joy and disbelief that God uses her in this way: 'I feel unworthy of it really.'

Occasionally the mockery of Christ is sharp. Around Easter time, one man stretched out his arms to form a crucifix and said, 'Not my idea of a fun way to spend Easter.' But Pen isn't judgemental and doesn't expect people who don't know God to live by his rules.

People respect her. She's not one to stop anyone's mouth but on occasion her colleagues, sensing that a particularly rich anecdote is about to turn the air blue, curb it with the phrase, 'Not while Pen's here.' And, of course, from time to time she's mocked for being a bit 'old-fashioned' – 'Have another drink', 'Get a man' kind of stuff. Every worldview has its evangelists. And then folk are mildly shocked to discover that she will have a lager from time to time and that she's reading a book about a group of contract killers going after five SAS men. And murdering four of them.

Sometimes it saddens her that some people put her in a box: 'We Christians are obviously a strange breed to them. And sometimes I feel like a bit of an alien.'

She pauses.

'But that, I suppose, is what we are.'

## Christian by design
## or
## A working hero is something to be

Brett is a graphic designer. Thirty-three and stopped count-
ing. He started out on his own, working freelance, taking his
work round to show people. Getting rejected. Getting
accepted. Today he is one of the directors of a smallish
design and printing company that has survived the reces-
sion. Just. He works hard and long. Often for some of the
weekend. He is well-off but doesn't have lots left over for
weekend trips to San Moritz. He is married to Page, and
they have four children and a three-bedroom semi full of
love and life and stuff and lots of people.

Brett is a Christian. He's also pretty determined and
gets up at around five to spend time with God. Up to an
hour, depending on when the kids explode into life. On the
way to work he listens to the music that's out there – REM,
Grant Lee Buffalo, Van Morrison, whatever – and from time
to time a music scripture memory tape. In the middle of
the day he does weights. And looks like it. I'm always polite
to Brett.

He has been to Bible College and has a good degree in
theology. He's putting it to use at work in the way he does
it, in the way he treats his clients, in the way he helps his
people when they've got a problem. And he's putting it to
work in his family and in running one of his church's youth
groups – forty to fifty teenagers, lots of pizza, houseparties,
summer outreach cafes in the local high street and serious,
well-thought-out, no-holds-barred Bible studies that give
the lie to the idea that all you can give teenagers is spiritual
jelly and ice-cream.

Now *there's* a model for our time.

After all, more teenagers are likely to end up as family
people with secular jobs than as full-time ministers in a
church.

He's not the only model, of course, but even if the Bretts of this world are largely unsung heroes, Paul, the great missionary, would probably have approved. He, after all, spent a fair chunk of his life making tents for a living.

• • •

# ANOTHER DAY, ANOTHER DIME?

### or
### A short theology of work

*The Christian community has a specific task ... to regain the lost sense of work as a divine calling.*

Emil Brunner

*Nothing is work unless you would rather be doing something else.*

William James

## THE WORKER GOD

In the beginning God...

Then he started work.

The Bible describes creation as the work of God. For six days he worked, and on the seventh he rested from all the work he had done. God is a worker, and work was something he chose to do. Part of his plan. Consistent with his holy nature. And as he considered his work at its various stages, he pronounced it good. Good after he made light, good after the third day, and the fourth and the fifth. And very good, as he considered all he had done.

· God's work is obviously distinguished from our work by the fact that he is all-powerful and his work is perfect, but his work of creation did involve many functions we think of as work:

- He makes things, as a craftsman might.

- He categorises and names things, as a zoologist might.

- He carries out his work in a clearly planned order; not all at once, it seems – the water and the sky have to wait three days for the fish and the birds, the land three days for the animals.

- He examines the quality of his work at every stage, as a fine artist or responsible manufacturer might.

- He assigns clearly defined functions to the components of creation, as a good engineer might – the greater light to govern the day and the lesser light to govern the night.

- He assigns a clearly defined role for humanity and provides the resources to fulfil that role, as a good manager might.

Furthermore, God's work reflects who he is. He creates humanity in his own image. We may not have his logo on us but all humanity bears his stamp, as perhaps we would like our work to do. A letter immaculately typed. A component faultlessly tooled. Something we want to be associated with.

Finally, God takes pleasure in his work, as perhaps we all do when a job is well done. When he's finished, he says that it is 'very good'.

So the Bible introduces us to God as the Creator, and describes his involvement in creation as his work. Work that he does voluntarily, with pleasure and satisfaction.

## BEFORE THE FALL

God gives humanity work to do. Humanity is designed for work – the work of subduing the earth and ruling over the animal world. This work is clearly given as a blessing:

> God blessed them and said to them, 'Be fruitful and increase in number; fill the earth and subdue it. Rule over the fish of the sea and the birds of the air and over every living creature that moves on the ground.'
>
> *Genesis 1:28*

> The Lord God took the man and put him in the Garden of Eden to work it and take care of it.
>
> *Genesis 2:15*

It is interesting to note that God gives two commands – not just to work the garden, but also to take care of it. There is in this command the human obligation to preserve the earth, not simply to exploit it for our own ends. Bulldozing Brazilian rain forests, working the soil to exhaustion for three years and then leaving it as a wasteland is not a biblical option.

The main point for our purposes is to note that work is not a consequence of the Fall but part of the original plan. We were always meant to work. And work was intended as a source of satisfaction and pleasure.

## AFTER THE FALL

When humanity rebelled against God the character of work changed. It would never be so easy again: 'By the sweat of your brow you will eat your food' (Gen 3:19).

Nevertheless, this didn't change the command to rule over the earth and subdue it. It didn't change the command to work, nor the essential value of work.

Indeed, God didn't simply banish Adam from Eden: he banished him *and* told him 'to work the ground from which he had been taken' (Gen 3:23). And although there would be toil, that didn't mean there would be no satisfaction in work. The pain women bear in child-birth would increase, but that didn't mean there would be no joy in having children. All creation was marred by Adam's sin, but the earth is still beautiful and the psalmist can still write with wonder, 'The heavens declare the glory of God; the skies proclaim the work of his hands' (Psalm 19:1). There is punishment but also grace. The command to work is maintained even if the way the work is done is radically altered.

The connection between God as worker and human-ity as workers is further stressed by the call to imitate God in the shape of the working week – God worked six days and then rested on the seventh, at least from the work of creation. Humanity is to do the same. This sug-gests that one way in which we reflect the image of God is in our work. And that work, in Genesis at least, is directly connected to looking after what he has created.

The affirmation of work pervades scripture. Even Ecclesiastes, a book not noted for its optimism, affirms it:

> This is what I have seen to be good: it is fitting to
> eat and drink and find enjoyment in all the toil
> with which one toils under the sun the few days
> of the life God gives us; for this is our lot.
>
> *Ecclesiastes 5:18, New Revised Standard Version*

The writer goes on to say that to be happy in one's work is 'a gift of God' and through work God keeps a person occupied with 'gladness of heart' (vs19–20,, NIV). He is not, however, under any illusions. He still describes work as 'toilsome labour under the sun'. So the fact that there can be satisfaction in work is not to say that work is always pleasurable or that periods of frustration and boredom at work are signs of divine displeasure. However, it is to state that work is a legitimate source of satisfaction and a divinely ordained part of the human condition.

Work, then, isn't man's idea: it is God's. Work is not an intermission from the main action, something we do so that we can then do other things, it is an integral part of the main action, an intrinsic part of our walk with God.

## THE LIMITS OF WORK

Nevertheless, the Old Testament as a whole puts limits on the significance of work. Ecclesiastes recognises that *in itself* work does not have ultimate value:

> My heart took delight in all my work,
>     and this was the reward for all my labour.
> Yet when I surveyed all that my hands had
>
>                                   done
>     and what I had toiled to achieve,
> everything was meaningless, a chasing after the
>
>                                   wind...
>
>                                   *Ecclesiastes 2:10–11*

If we look for our significance in our work, we will come away with empty hearts. Our significance lies in our relationship with the Creator of work.

Similarly, Exodus and Deuteronomy put work in perspective and set clear limits to the amount of time we spend working – six days. The seventh was to be the Sabbath – a rest day. And the command not to work on that day finds expression throughout the Old Testament. Several reasons are given for the command:

- So that we can acknowledge God as Creator honouring his designation of the Sabbath as a blessed and holy day.

- So that we can rest.
- So that we can allow others to rest as a way of preventing their exploitation.

## STOP, IN THE NAME OF GOD

God is the Lord of time, and time is a gift of God to us. On the seventh day he called the Israelites to set aside their time to him. Today we need to set aside the frantic drive to put every day, every minute, to profitable use, to meet our agenda and slake our thirst for the security we think we can find in constant activity. Time is what many of us feel we don't have enough of, so there is always the temptation to break the rhythm of work and rest that God lays down.

The command to rest applied not only to the Israelites but also to foreigners who worked for them. Deuteronomy 5:15 reinforces the command to give slaves the day off by reminding the people of their experience of tyrannical slavery in Egypt. The people of God must not exercise power in a similar way.

Limits are set on material gain: the people of God are to keep the Sabbath even when the time to accomplish the work is limited.

> '…on the seventh day you shall rest; even during the ploughing season and harvest you must rest.'
>
> *Exodus 34:21*

Don't work on the Sabbath – even though the seeds may be planted too late, the rain may come and the harvest may go rotten. Humanity needs to recognise God as the provider, to put him before greed, to set aside anxiety and put limits on gainful labour. There is no room for the materialism that drives people to a seven-day week. Nor is there room for the workaholism that turns work into an idol which determines the entire shape of one's life. This pushes God out and puts work in first place.

In Old Testament thought, the Sabbath becomes a crucial indicator of fidelity to the God of Israel. In Isaiah 56, the Lord promises his blessing on those who maintain justice and do what is right, who stop their hands from doing evil and keep the Sabbath without desecrating it. Keeping the Sabbath is the only specific mentioned amongst a number of general exhortations to live in line with God's character. Similarly, God promises a memorial and a name to the eunuchs 'who keep my Sabbaths, who choose what pleases me and hold fast to my covenant' (Isa 56:4). Again in verse 6 God's promise of his blessing on foreigners is based on their overall commitment and love for God *and* the keeping of the Sabbath.

The New Testament clarifies this teaching in one vitally important way. The key text is Mark 2:27: 'The sabbath was made for humankind, and not humankind for the sabbath...' (NRSV).

In other words, the Sabbath is there for *our* benefit. It is intended as a blessing, not a means of preventing rest and refreshment. That said, the New Testament releases us from the *command* to dedicate one day to God. The new life in Christ is life in the Spirit, so there is the freedom to discern prayerfully how to apply the principle of rest, of giving God time, of not worshipping work, of setting limits on the time we spend working for money.

Nevertheless, these principles should, in my view, be applied. We may be released from the mandate to take a particular day off, but we are surely unwise to ignore the principles our Creator has laid down for our benefit.

## WORK AS WORSHIP

The New Testament, like the Old, affirms the value of work. Jesus was a carpenter by trade. Manual labour is a dignified occupation not just for the son of Joseph but for the Son of God. Work is both necessary and good. God doesn't take the Christian out of the world; rather, he transforms all aspects of life in the world. Including work. In line with this, Paul calls on Christians to do their work for God. Work becomes one of the ways humanity serves God. It becomes a component of our worship. Interestingly, Hebrew uses the same word for 'worship' as for 'work' – *avodah*. The English word 'service' perhaps comes closest to capturing both meanings.

Work, then, is worship. It is done for God and, as we shall see later, this has radical implications for our attitude to the quality of our performance.

## WHAT IS WORK?

In our age work has increasingly been defined in economic terms. Work is what you are paid to do. You are not working if you are not earning a wage. And you have less status if you are not working. This applies not just to the unemployed but to people like housewives and househusbands, who don't receive a wage for their efforts. Indeed, one of the most tragic cries of Western culture is 'Oh, I'm just a housewife'.

When you ask the chairman of IBM what he does, he doesn't say, 'Oh, I'm *just* the chairman of IBM.' When you are introduced to the Archbishop of Canterbury, he doesn't say, 'Oh, I'm *just* the Archbishop of Canterbury.'

The person who tells you she is 'just a housewife' is probably communicating two things.

1  She doesn't think you think her work is very significant.

2  She doesn't think her work is very significant either.

Why? Because it's not paid? Because it is repetitive? Because it involves a lot of tasks that are perceived as not requiring a great deal of skill? Forty years ago being a 'homemaker' was a highly respected and valued form of work. The devaluation of the role highlights the need to be wary of definitions of work that relate to a particular culture.

The Bible resists a definition of work that relates merely to earning a wage. Making beds and cleaning floors is work not only when it is done by a paid auxiliary in a hospital, it is work when it is done by a housewife or househusband. Plumbing in a washing machine is not just work when it is done by a professional plumber, it is work when Mum does it at the weekend after a long week in the sales office.

So definitions of what constitutes rest may vary from person to person. It might mean, for example, that a housewife should be relieved of the cooking one day a week. It is, after all, what she does every day. Cooking is part of her contribution to the economic process, allowing her partner to leave the home to earn money.

Should she 'cease' from this task? One characteristic of the Sabbath does seem to be a change in the nature of activity from the other six days – that is, stopping what one does most of the time. Indeed, the Hebrew word for Sabbath means 'to stop or cease'. So work might be defined as the activities you are principally engaged in during the week, whether in or out of the home, 'employed' or 'unemployed'.

## WORKING FOR OURSELVES, WORKING FOR OTHERS

Work certainly includes what we do to provide for ourselves and those we are responsible for:

> If anyone does not provide for his relatives, and especially for his immediate family, he has denied the faith and is worse than an unbeliever.
>
> *1 Timothy 5:8*

This is a remarkably strong statement and could easily lead to false guilt, particularly for those who are unemployed through no fault of their own. However, Paul was writing for a community where work was available. That said, his statement reveals how important it is to create a society where it is possible for people to provide for their own and their family's material needs. Denying someone the ability to provide for their family is to deny them a fundamental form of human expression.

Work includes any activity that contributes to the provision of human needs – cooking, washing, food shopping, car maintenance – as well as those activities that generate money directly. The purposes of work, however, extend beyond simple material provision for ourselves and our immediate family:

- We work so we can give to those who don't have. Note Paul's remarkable statement about the necessity for reformed thieves to work so that they can give to those in need (Eph 4:28).

- We work to serve others, to improve life for the community as a whole. The baker baking bread, the car manufacturer making cars, the writer writing, the 'housespouse' teaching her child to walk, the nurse caring for a patient – all contribute to the quality of community life.

- We work to develop gifts and skills, to express ourselves through the tasks we do, to gain the satisfaction of a job well done, to rejoice in our God-given abilities.

Provision, service, personal development – all good reasons to work. But none of them good reasons to turn work into an idol, to sacrifice our friends and families at its all-consuming altar, to say that the extra work is being done for the good of the family, when in fact the family is being destroyed by the workaholism of absentee parents. God created humanity for relationship with him and with one another. He created work as a blessing for us, as a means of provision and mutual service. He did not create us to be slaves of work.

Nevertheless, in a society where some people seem to have too much work to do and others have none at all, in a society where many live in fear of unemployment and many others live in despair of ever finding paid work, keeping work in godly perspective is no easy job.

# • 3 •

# WINNING AWAY

## or
## How to avoid a split personality

*I can do everything through him who gives me
strength.*

Philippians 4:13

In most sports it's harder to win away from home. The
rules don't change, you don't change, the opposition
doesn't change. But the ground changes, and there is a
psychological disadvantage in playing in front of predominantly hostile supporters.

We know that our God's character doesn't change.
We know that our God is love. But are we convinced
that his love is as much directed to the people at ICI as
the people at St Michael's? As much concerned for
Welsh miners as Papuan tribesmen?

God loves people constantly, all day and all night.
Weekdays and Sundays. He loves them when they're in
the factory and when they're not in the factory.

God is at work at work. His identity doesn't change.
He's in the business of completing his purposes in us

and through us. In and through the people around us. Home and away. At home. At work.

The Bible tells us that Jesus Christ is the same yesterday, today and forever. He died to give us abundant life. And this abundant life is ours not only when we're at at home, or in Bible studies, or in church services, but in our life as a secretary, or a nurse, or a mechanic, or a stockbroker. There is no division. If the Christian life doesn't work nine to five, then maybe it's no more than a nice leisure activity like aerobics, golf or crocheting.

God's identity doesn't change after nine.

And our identity doesn't change either.

## PRINCE OR PAUPER?

You may think you are a computer programmer, a waitress, an editor, an engineer, a cook. You are – and you are also something very grand. You are a child of God (John 1:12). A child of the King. A prince or princess. This idea has always rather appealed to me, especially since my idea of a prince is so firmly rooted in historical fables – a noble, courageous, compassionate paragon of virtue, with a flowing red velvet cape and a black stallion. Irresistible. Wishful thinking on my part, I'm afraid. Nevertheless, we are royalty.

It may not feel that way. In fact, it may feel the opposite. We may feel abused, unappreciated, a dispensable cog in a heartless machine. But our essential identity in Christ is not changed by how people treat us.

> Therefore, if anyone is in Christ, he is a new creation; the old has gone, the new has come!
>
> *2 Corinthians 5:17*

We are a new creation, and *Christ is in us*. The Christian's identity doesn't change according to his circumstances. We don't become secularised, despiritualised, unholy when we are in the workplace. We are still new creatures, still a royal priesthood, still heirs of marvellous promises, still called to holiness, still promised the power to resist temptation, still promised the fruit of the Spirit. Certainly we may have a different role at work, but that doesn't make us different people. Nevertheless, to be consistent we need to call on God's help to live according to our true identity, whatever the pressure. Easier written than done, but God has provided the resources.

We go to work with God's authority and in his power. We go to work as his ambassadors with his message. We need to have confidence in those resources and in that message.

> So we are ambassadors for Christ, since God is
> making his appeal through us…
>
> *2 Corinthians 5:20, NRSV*

Today probably more than 95% of British people don't know Jesus in a personal way. God makes his appeal through us.

Today many of our major institutions are strongholds of secular humanist thought. Strongholds that can be taken captive to obey Christ:

> The weapons we fight with are not the weapons
> of the world. On the contrary, they have divine
> power to demolish strongholds. We demolish
> arguments and every pretension that sets itself up
> against the knowledge of God, and we take cap-
> tive every thought to make it obedient to Christ.
>
> *2 Corinthians 10:4–5*

This vision of strong Christian corporate influence may seem like a fantasy in the pressure and hurly-burly of the everyday, but we do need to be careful before we dismiss it. After all, who would have thought that a servant of the living God would become a pagan empire's chief administrator? This is what happened to Daniel, who began his career as just one of a group of talented Israelite youths deported to Babylon and, without compromising his faith, was subsequently promoted to head of the civil service. The whole empire may not in Daniel's time have bowed down to the God of Israel, but it was run in a way that reflected Daniel's reliance on the wisdom of the words and ways of the God of Abraham, Isaac and Jacob. Wisdom that caused Darius, his boss, to seek to promote him to chief administrator of the entire empire and then, after the incident in the lions' den, to protect the religious rights of the Jewish people: 'I issue a decree that in every part of my kingdom people must fear and reverence the God of Daniel' (Dan 6:26).

The God of Daniel is our God. As Darius put it...

'For he is the living God
    and he endures for ever;
his kingdom will not be destroyed,
    his dominion will never end.
He rescues and he saves;
    he performs signs and wonders
in the heavens and on the earth.
He has rescued Daniel
    from the power of the lions.'

*Daniel 6:26–27*

Certainly many great companies and institutions were founded by Christians and have been run on Christian principles: Rowntree's, Cadbury's, Lloyd's, Barclay's, Huntley & Palmer's – to name but five established by Quaker families. There's no particular reason why the same cannot happen today.

Maybe not everyone in your workplace will become

a Christian, but perhaps you can work and pray to see it run on lines that reflect justice, mercy and respect for other people so that your co-workers will, like Darius, give praise to the living God.

## CLOCKING ON WITH GOD

The issue for us is that our God and our identities don't change when we walk through the factory gates. Indeed, it may well be that to be fruitful ministers in our workplace we don't actually need any startling new ideas. Rather, we simply need to apply what we already know from other areas of our life to our workplace.

Samson discovered that the Spirit of God was just as powerful on Philistine territory as he was within the borders of Israel. Indeed, he discovered that the Spirit of God had just as much freedom to work in the very temple of the Philistine idol Dagon as he did in Judah (Judg 16:23–30). But do *we* feel that God is as powerful in the factory as in church? As much Emmanuel, God with us, at work as at home?

Jacob, fleeing from the revenge of his brother, beds down on the road to Haran with a stone for a pillow. God appears to him in a dream and confirms the promises he had made to his father and grandfather. Waking, Jacob says, 'Surely the Lord is in this place, and I was not aware of it' (Gen 28:16). Perhaps like Jacob we need to wake up and realise that God hasn't abandoned us at the factory gate like some parent dropping off his child at school. He is there. He is with us. And our resources are in no way diminished.

Surely, God is in your workplace. Are you aware of it?

Surely, God's promises still apply.

Surely, God is with you there.

As he is with you everywhere.

# • 4 •

# THE CAMOMILE FACTOR

## or
### Building relationships in love

*We must not, in thinking about how we can make a
big difference, ignore the small daily differences we
can make which, over time, add up to big differences
we often cannot foresee.*

Marian Wright Edelman

Before you read this chapter, you may want to consider
writing down the names of three people with whom you
believe God wants you to develop a deeper relationship.

## WIMPS AND WEIRDOS?

Christians don't have a very good image. On TV, clergy
are often portrayed as well-meaning, bumbling, absent-
minded, slightly overweight, giggly wimps with secret
weaknesses for sherry or cream cakes. The reality of the
non-Christian's view is probably bleaker. Who, for
example is describing whom in these research results?

These people are...
Less free
More unfashionable

More isolated
Less sexually fulfilled
More boring
Psychologically weaker
With fewer interests
Less realistic
Less involved in the real world
Less happy
Less friendly...

That's the opinion of Newcastle students about Christians (from S M Boice, *Negative Attitudes to Christianity*).

Building trust is vital in any relationship. And one barrier to developing trust is the preconceptions that many non-Christians have about Christians. So it is important to understand and face the non-Christian's attitude to Christians.

Here's how I think the average non-Christian working in London perceives the average Christian:

Boring. They don't drink, don't dance, don't swear. They pretend not to have sex. They don't know how to have fun, so they are trying to ruin it for the rest of us. They give away their money and go to church on Sundays as if it were a social club. Frankly, my golf club is more fun. And it's cheaper. The whole thing is a crutch. They are stupid and simple-minded. How can anyone really believe that stuff? It's superstitious mumbo jumbo. What's worse is that they're constantly trying to stuff it down our throats. Why should I accept it — I don't see any difference in their lives — Catholics, Protestants, born-again, whatever. They're either fanatics or saccharine sweet. No spine. I've met one or two neat Christians, it's true, but most of them are weird. If that's what

> happens to Christians, it's not a club I want to
> join. What would my friends think?

That is pretty much what I thought about Christians before I became one. A huddle of mushy, simple-minded, ineffectual, well-meaning, boring, hypocritical, weird people. Sometimes the attitude still persists in me – and in others. For example, a while ago someone said to me of another Christian, 'I like spending time with her – I want to build up my base of Christians who are normal.'

If we are going to witness effectively, we need to be aware of the preconceptions that non-Christians hold. We need to recognise that there is some truth in those preconceptions and to prepare ourselves to deal with them. At the same time, we need to prepare ourselves to be thought weird, hypocritical and simple-minded. And not to care.

## SILENT LIGHT?

Still, if some non-Christians are suspicious, some are utterly indifferent. And others quite open. In any event, we need to understand where they are coming from. And to determine that, whatever their views, we will neither become paranoid nor allow ourselves to be intimidated into silence. Of course, silence may for a while – even a long while – be the way the Spirit leads you. The path of silent witness should, however, not be the product of fear but rather the fruit of closeness to God.

Our understanding of our co-workers' suspicion and their fear of being trapped by a Christian fanatic should make us careful how we talk about church and church-related activities. It may make us careful about bringing up religion before we have established a basis for friendship. But we should never let this stop us talking about Christ in a natural way. Most people can tolerate a little talk about Jesus. We simply need to know how and when to change the subject. Particularly perhaps in the early stages of a relationship, a swift change of topic can build tremendous trust. A non-Christian probably expects you to have the tenacity of a bulldog once the subject of religion comes up. Not pushing it early on may well give her the confidence to raise it herself, or not to be put off if you mention it some other time.

## CONTAMINATING COLLEAGUES?

It is important not just that we recognise what our non-Christian co-workers think of Christians, but that we recognise what we, in turn, really think of them. What is our view of their lifestyle?

Superficial, self-destructive, empty, unfulfilling, contaminating? Something to flee from? Something to be afraid of? The consequence of such thinking is that many mature Christians retreat into a Christian ghetto, into splendid isolation. Most of their friends are Christians. Almost all their disposable time is spent with Christians. This attitude impairs evangelism in two ways:

1   Christians don't spend time with non-Christians outside the workplace, so non-Christians are not exposed as much to the love of the gospel.

2   Non-Christians in the workplace sense the distance, sense the judgement that is being passed on them by Christians. This builds a barrier.

And how often do Christians avoid going to clubs and discos, not because they are dens of iniquity (though some of them are) or because they have developed a conviction about not dancing, but because they don't know how to dance and therefore feel uncomfortable?

How often do we avoid inviting someone over for supper, not because we don't like him, but because we think he'll find our Christian friends boring and we'll have nothing to talk about?

## DOWN WITH THE BARRIERS

The barrier to building relationships with non-Christians is often *not* their debauchery, but our fear, our neuroses, our inadequacies, our fear of rejection, of embarrassment, of being thought weird, of having nothing to talk about. We have to get right with ourselves, we have to recognise that we are worthy. This will give us the confidence to meet non-Christians on their own ground, as Christ did. We have to realise God loves them just the way they are. *And* that he loves us just the way we are.

Often the non-Christian will test us, will tell incredibly filthy jokes or swear more than usual, just to see how we will react. Will we crumble under the onslaught? Will we condemn him? Perhaps there is sometimes a need to challenge, but often the most effective method is simply not to behave in the same way yourself.

Ted Cobden was a Christian who worked with me. When he joined, he was very junior and very mature in God. Almost from his first day, before anybody knew he was a Christian, nobody swore round him – despite his lowly rank. Why? Ted never rebuked anybody. Mainly I think people just sensed something about him, something gentle and tender. And perhaps, subconsciously at first, they noticed he didn't swear. The power of example.

## CHRIST AT WORK

In developing relationships, Christ's example is instructive. His behaviour was often startlingly at odds with the culture surrounding him. For example, three things non-Christians believe about Christians are:

1 They go to church.
2 They don't drink.
3 They choose their friends wisely.

But what did Christ do?

1 He was accused of breaking the Sabbath.
2 He drank wine.
3 He went to parties with publicans and sinners (Mark 2:15–17).

Indeed, at the gathering described in Mark's Gospel, there is no record of Jesus sharing the Good News. He spent time with people – on their territory. And what is interesting is that they invited him. They seemed to like having him around. He obviously didn't inhibit them, or judge them, or sit in a corner to avoid contamination. Jesus was able to break the conventions of the religious leaders around him, without sinning. Similarly, some of us will need to question whether the church conventions that make us feel there are certain places we can't go are actually ones we should continue to follow. The pub is, after all, one of the main places people meet in our culture. Going for a drink, albeit a Perrier, at lunchtime may be precisely the right way to develop a relationship with a co-worker. That said, there is an important issue of conscience here and those who don't feel able to shouldn't. And shouldn't be made to feel guilty.

Beyond understanding our co-workers, there is the call to serve them. Let's look at the way Jesus serves non-believers.

In John 5, he takes the initiative, and approaches and heals a paralytic, but doesn't identify himself. He helps out with a physical problem.

In John 6, he feeds five thousand people. He takes on a responsibility that is clearly not his any more than it would be your responsibility to feed five thousand people who happened to crash your picnic in Hyde Park.

Yes, Jesus preaches and teaches, but he also takes initiatives and meets people's needs.

## MINISTRY MEETS NEEDS

What are the needs of people around you at work? Do you know? What are the felt needs of the three people you have written down? Well, here are some of the things that Christians at my old company were ministering to, some of the problems their co-workers were facing:

Divorce
Cancer in the family
A husband's heart attack
The end of a love affair
A decision about marriage
A 35-year-old psychological problem
An invisible, but incurable, sexually transmitted
     disease
Separation
Bringing up a child as an unmarried mother

Today the list would almost certainly include:

Money
Debt
Fear of unemployment

We relate to people at work primarily through our work. But we must not forget that they are people, and we must not flee from their pain.

Ministry is love in action. Ministry is bringing the whole gospel – in all its power and light and love – into the workplace. When a minister sees a need, he seeks to meet it. The parable of the good Samaritan is, after all, not only a response to the question 'Who is my neighbour?' but also an answer to the unposed question 'Who is a minister?' And you are the minister.

Ministry is love in action, and love, according to 1 Corinthians 14:1, is our aim. All the skills in the world will make little impact unless we have genuine concern for our neighbours who don't know Jesus.

And our neighbour is the lady at the next word-processor, the man in the next office, the person behind the cafeteria check-out, our boss...

## TAKING THE INITIATIVE — WITH LOVE

Observing particular needs isn't enough. Some observations can be turned into prayer. In other cases we need to take initiatives to build trust.

Initiative is very important. We cannot sit back and expect people to come to us. Jesus consistently took the initiative. He went to people, he asked questions, he came to die for us. We didn't invite him.

Love takes the initiative. And lovers are extremely creative and resourceful. Love goes to every shop in town to find the chocolates she adores. Love finds the right card. Love makes time.

## THE CAMOMILE FACTOR

Here are two examples of people taking the initiative to communicate love, to build relationships.

Craig Miller, a banker, decided he would get a colleague in his department a birthday cake, stick a candle on it, and go and make a fuss of him. Unprecedented in that particular bank. It just wasn't done. But who could object to a birthday cake? The Christian breaking down cultural barriers, gently pushing at the conventions that depersonalise the working environment. The Christian saying, 'It need not be this way.'

Emily, a small Chinese lady, works at the United Nations. One day one of her co-workers, a fairly large lady, wasn't feeling well.

'Can I get you a cup of tea?' Emily enquired.

'No,' the other replied rather shortly, 'I don't like the tea here. I only drink camomile.'

Emily left her, quietly slipped on her coat, took the lift down several floors and went down the street to a nearby shop. She returned with a box of camomile tea and gave it in her small hand to this large lady, who immediately enveloped her in a huge hug, exclaiming, 'Emily, I love you.'

Emily replied, rather muffled from the epicentre of this massive hug, 'I love you too.'

Emily's story illustrates a number of important points:

- **Be ministry minded – listen.** Emily could have just smiled and gone on her way. Instead, because she is ministry-minded, because she listened, because she saw the other person's need and desire, she took an initiative that totally transformed another person's mood and day.

- **Time is on *your* side, the opportunities will come.** We don't have to create situations in which we can minister. They will happen all by themselves. We are going to be in the workplace for a long time, we don't need to be anxious about finding opportunities. We simply have to pray and be alert.

- **Ministry is to individual people.** Obviously, camomile tea wouldn't have been a good idea for everyone. We have talked about general principles and stereotypical non-Christian attitudes to the Christian. But each of us deals with individuals, so we must seek to study the habits, needs and desires of those individuals. It is going to be different in each case.

How much do you know about the three people you have written down? What is their favourite food? Their favourite hobby? How do they like their coffee? What is their most serious concern?

• **Ministry doesn't demand, it gives.** Emily asked for nothing, not even the money for the tea. Like the good Samaritan she simply gave, expecting nothing in return. Our expressions of love for others shouldn't have evangelistic strings attached. Emily didn't give the lady a Bible with the tea, or use it as an excuse to invite her to a Bible study. We must be tactful and sensitive as we love, and distinguish between the opportunities to serve and the opportunities to communicate the gospel verbally.

But do think about these little things. A thank-you note. An apology for a sharp word. Asking forgiveness isn't only a biblical imperative, it is also so rare that it is an extremely powerful witness – though naturally, we shouldn't do it just for that reason. A note of encouragement in someone's top drawer. A flower. A polo. The offer of a cup of coffee. A card for Easter. For the Chinese New Year. A newspaper clipping on a favourite topic. The offer, if someone is working late, to help out or to go get a sandwich. Food is almost always helpful. And, at the appropriate time, you can become just a little bolder.

For example, a lady called Jill, who worked for me and who had only just become a Christian, used to buy our boss his morning bran muffin on her way into work. One day she left a verse with it, presumably on the theory that man cannot live by bran muffin alone. She just didn't know that you are not meant to witness to your boss's boss, so she did. A small act, but at the time a very brave one. A risk – he might have been offended. She judged right and God was gracious. He wasn't offended.

Then she invited him to read the Bible with her. She just didn't know that baby Christians are not meant to do that. It wasn't long before our boss became a believer. A little step. Take one.

These are the little everyday things that transform the work environment, that turn it into a place people enjoy. We should be diligent in expressing love. Is there some little thing you could do for someone next week?

## LOVE IN ACTION

The interesting thing about these little things is that they catch on. People start to follow suit. Don't worry that this is not directly communicating the plan of salvation. Remember you are an expression of the gospel and, when you put a mint on someone's desk, you communicate 1 John 3:18:

> Dear children, let us not love in words or tongue but with actions and in truth.

When you don't grumble and complain, you communicate Philippians 2:14–16:

> Do everything without complaining or arguing, so that you may become blameless and pure, children of God without fault in a crooked and depraved generation, in which you shine like stars in the universe as you hold out the word of life...

And you communicate these verses in a form that cannot be tuned out. The non-Christian can ignore almost every direct communication of the gospel. But he cannot ignore you wandering around filled with the fruit of the Spirit (Gal 5:22–23).

Sometimes you can give someone a book that has a Christian perspective on an issue they are dealing with – bereavement, raising kids, depression in the family, who to marry, whether to stay married. It may not be C S Lewis' *Mere Christianity*, but it may clearly show them how relevant and helpful the Bible is to the everyday problems of life. One evening I was leaving the office and, in the lift, met someone who used to work with me. We chatted. She told me she was trying to work out whether to marry this man who had proposed to her.

By coincidence perhaps, I happened to have with me a copy of Jack and Carole Mayhall's *Marriage Takes More than Love*. I gave it to her. I saw her again on Monday. She had read the whole thing, had accepted its perspective on marriage, though not on the gospel, and it had helped her to see why this particular man wasn't right for her. She wanted a copy for him.

By coincidence perhaps, I happened to have another one with me.

They didn't get married. And, as far as I know, she hasn't yet become a Christian. But I hope that the seed planted will bear fruit, that one day she will remember that when she needed wisdom for her life, she got it from a book based on the Bible. I couldn't have given her a Bible at that point, but I could give her something relevant to her life situation.

So, take initiatives in love.

## USING THE WAY YOU WORK

Obviously not everyone could have left their office as Emily did to go and buy camomile tea. The culture changes from office to office, but in each situation there are probably times and opportunities that are particularly conducive to developing relationships.

In my own case the way we worked was very helpful for developing good relationships. I spent a lot of time in meetings with people, a lot of time travelling with people, and a lot of time with my immediate boss and those working with me. So I got to know them quite well. And I had my own office, so it was easy to talk more personally if that was the way the conversation turned. At some stages in my career lunchtime provided a regular opportunity to spend time with people. At others I had to work through lunch, or my schedule was too unpredictable to make arrangements. Our circumstances change. But are we looking for opportunities?

Mark is a lawyer who spends most of his time working on his own. There are not many meetings, and he doesn't travel. How does he develop relationships? He is going to have to take deliberate steps to make time to get to know his co-workers.

Craig is a banker. He works in an open-plan office which makes it hard to let conversations flow into personal areas. However, he does travel, and lunch is a good time for him to develop relationships with those around him.

When are the times in your workplace when it is appropriate to develop relationships? Is it after work over a drink? Do you need to join one of the company sports teams? Or determine to have lunch with one of your three people once a month? Do pray about what initiatives you could take to build trusting relationships.

# • 5 •

# EDGE WITHOUT GUILT

## or
## Getting the message out

*She was reading her Bible in the canteen. Which is a
pretty brave thing to do. People think you're a nut-
head if you're a Christian.*

Katriina Greene, nurse

## • SNAPSHOT •
## Clumsy for Christ

Five of us were on a two-day trip out of town. Surely with
all that time God would give me an opportunity to share
something with someone. No opportunity came, or at least
none that I could see. The time came to fly home.

The client and I decided to work together on the plane.
So, briefcase in hand, I negotiated my way into the window
seat. As I lifted my case over the seat-rest, the lid came open
and out tumbled about twenty small orange booklets…'

'Oh no,' I thought. Twenty copies of a tract called 'The
Four Spiritual Laws' scattered over the floor and on the
seats in front of me and my client. I felt like a teenager caught
with some improper publication. I began to pick them up.

Then the very worst thing that could have happened actually happened.

The client said, 'What are those?'

'Errrrrrrrrrrrrrrrrrrrrrrrr... They're little booklets which explain the main points about Christianity.'

I waited for a look of embarrassment. Or perhaps pity. Or discomfort.

'Oh, that's interesting,' she said, with a genuinely interested and open expression on her face. 'I've been thinking a lot about that recently. Could I have a look?'

• • •

## THE GREAT DREAD

Witnessing is a guilt-edged word that fills many Christians with dread, particularly in the context of secular employment. Some of this dread has to do with natural nervousness, fear of rejection or lack of confidence.

Some of this dread may also have to do with an incomplete understanding of witnessing as simply the verbal delivery of the gospel message, telling someone what the gospel is and challenging them to accept it. It is that. Or at least that is a critical component of witnessing and something we often try to avoid. But witnessing is more than just that. It is living the gospel in such a way that the difference it makes is communicated non-verbally. We witness verbally to the truth of the life, death, resurrection and ascension of Jesus. But we witness in deed and in character to the transformation that has occurred in our lives through what he has done for us.

Jesus makes a difference. Unlike Muhammad, Jesus didn't simply come to *bring* a message – he *was* the message. The word made flesh. And witnessing to him is living that message in our human flesh. It is being and doing and speaking.

## SEEING IS BELIEVING

The impact of the gospel is in significant measure communicated non-verbally as well as verbally. In his second letter to the Christians at Corinth, Paul says:

> You yourselves are our letter [of recommendation], written on our hearts, known and read by everybody. You show that you are a letter from Christ, the result of our ministry, written not with ink but with the Spirit of the living God, not on tablets of stone but on tablets of human hearts.
>
> *2 Corinthians 3:2–3*

We are letters of recommendation. When people read us, what do they see?

We are Christ's advertisements in our workplace. Are we ads that speak to people of the divine, that suggest there may be a better way? Or boring ads? That lack wit or boldness? As Marshall McLuhan said, the medium is the message, and we are the medium. What is our message?

It is not only what we say but what we are. Robert Murray McCheyne wrote this to pastors, but the principle applies to us all:

> Covet universal holiness of life. Your whole usefulness depends on this, for your sermons last but an hour or two; your life preaches all the week.

Our lives are under constant scrutiny at work. We spend more time there than anywhere else. We spend more time with co-workers than anyone else. They see when we succeed, when we fail, when we remain joyful in tough circumstances, when we cancel social engagements, when we are asked to work on Sundays, when we are promoted, when we are tired and hungry. Our lives preach all the week.

## HOLINESS AT WORK

The world we live in puts an emphasis on techniques rather than on character. On results, on instant gratification, on tangible manifestations of success, on methods to achieve that success, on 'how to'. How to be happy. How to bring up children. How to have a happy wife. How to have a happy husband.

Technique is important, but not nearly as important as holy character. And holiness is not primarily an ethereal, otherworldly quality of misty peacefulness and beatific grins. Rather, it is the obedience that springs from love of God and love of one's neighbour. Several times in Leviticus 18–20, God says, 'Be holy because I, the Lord your God, am holy', then goes on to give a string of commandments that relate to idolatry, the occult, telling the truth, justice, business practice, feeding the poor, protecting resident foreigners, and so on. Holiness works itself out in obedience to God across the whole range of human behaviour. Character works itself out in action. Both who we are and what we do are vital components of witnessing.

And don't believe that it is not having an impact.

## LEGAL EXPENSES

Lewis Trippett was a lawyer working for a telephone company. One day a woman came in from the accounts department. He had never seen her before. She asked him if he was Lewis Trippett. With some trepidation, he replied, 'Yes, I am.'

She said, 'You're the only one in this department with any integrity. Don't change. Everyone else abuses their expenses.'

Then she left as abruptly as she had come.

Little things make a difference.

In Matthew 5:16, Jesus says: 'In the same way, let

your light shine before men, that they may see your good deeds and praise your Father in heaven.'

Now, it does *not* say: 'Let your *good deeds* so shine before men that they may see your light and give glory to your Father in heaven.'

The emphasis is not on the deeds but on the light. This is a vital distinction. What we want people to see is the light and the true God behind it, not what *we* are doing. Similarly, John in his Gospel talks about Jesus' miracles as signs, pointers to his identity. The miraculous deeds point to the light.

Both Cain and Abel bring sacrifices to God. One brings sheep and one brings groceries. One is pleasing to God and one isn't. This has nothing to do with the produce but rather with the character of the man. It isn't just what we do but how we do it that determines the extent to which it brings glory to God.

## BEING 'FRANK'

In the building where I used to work there was a lift operator called Frank. He stood at the bank of lifts in the main entrance and ensured there was an even balance of lifts going up and lifts coming down. For many people this might be a menial, repetitive task with little opportunity to shine. But day in, day out, Frank would have a smile for everyone as they came in to work. Frank would greet us by name. He seemed to know all our names. And he would tell us to have love in our hearts.

Frank was a lift operator but people didn't see menial drudgery in his job. They saw in it an opportunity to transmit love and joy, to make people look forward to their day and help them overcome the frustrations of their journey into work. One person even walked round the block to come in at Frank's entrance so she could start her day with a warm welcome from Frank. I don't know whether Frank was a Christian, but people saw his job in the light of his cheerful, giving spirit. When he retired, my company gave him a significant chunk of our shares. And he didn't even work for us – he worked for the owner of our office building. He made a difference.

So it is with our work. In what light do we want it to be seen?

Ideally, we want people to see in our work the light Jesus has brought into our lives. What we do and the way we relate to people should point others to God. Excellence, which we will discuss later, does not in itself do that. Excellence is not necessarily the exclusive province of God's children – nor is good character, nor is honesty. Somehow, by grace, by the power of the Spirit to transform us, to work in us, there must be something about our light that points to God.

## PHARAOH'S PRAISE

Joseph is a good example. His discernment so shone before Pharaoh that Pharaoh gave him the name 'Zaphenath-Paneah', which means 'God is living'. Indeed, it is precisely because Pharaoh recognised God's revelation in Joseph's wisdom that he put Joseph in charge of Egypt:

> …Pharaoh asked [his officials], 'Can we find anyone like this man, one in whom is the spirit of God?'
>
> Then Pharaoh said to Joseph, 'Since God has made all this known to you, there is no-one so discerning and wise as you. You shall be in charge of my palace, and all my people are to submit to your orders.'
>
> Genesis 41:38–40

God's revelation of the meaning of Pharaoh's dreams was a one-off supernatural event, but it was followed by a lifetime of faithfulness and wisdom. Certainly God does intervene in supernatural ways as he did in Joseph's life, and we may or may not give him the glory. However, he also has the opportunity to reveal himself through our character, through our response to everyday events. Our lights can shine, our testimony to the power of the gospel can be powerful, without the direct verbal communication of the Good News.

How God is going to use you in the process of bringing those around you to himself is up to him and you. In one case you may do something that may not truly register for another decade; in another you may lead someone to the Lord. In another you may encounter some hostility. One person hoes, one person sows, one person waters. But he will use you, whether or not you are always aware of it.

Think for a moment of the way God brought you to himself. Certainly there may be one or two people who were particularly significant. And there may be people you have completely forgotten, who taught you something important. But maybe in heaven you will know the impact they had.

Equally, there are probably people who did things that struck you or people who said something that made a big impact on you. They will never know, at least not till heaven, the difference they made.

## VICTORY TEA

When I was a student and not yet a Christian, my college hockey team had an end-of-season tea. A couple of the team were Christians and they volunteered to host the occasion. They laid on a sumptuous feast. They also laid on something that I, at least, didn't expect. Maybe

I had missed an announcement or a note somewhere along the line. Anyway there we all were, twelve or thirteen hockey players, good and true – and up pops a missionary.

I was probably a little irritated. I suppose he must have given us a talk. I don't remember. What I do remember is that as the afternoon wore on we had a discussion about what happens to people who don't accept Christ as their Saviour. I used to love debates, and as the discussion progressed I sniffed blood with all the glee of a piranha in a Bond movie.

'So,' I said to the missionary, trying to conceal the thrill of anticipated triumph, 'what you're saying is that good rabbis go to hell.'

In the context of that gathering of people, this was a no-win situation for him.

If he said, 'Yes, they do', he would lose all credibility with the non-Christians present, or so I thought.

If he said 'No', then there was no need for a Jew like me to become a Christian.

If he pfaffed around and tried to duck the issue, he would be a pfaffer who had tried to duck the issue.

I can still remember the scene. He was sitting back in an armchair opposite me. He rubbed his left temple with his left hand and looked down at the floor. I waited on the edge of my seat. And then in reply he said softly, almost sadly, 'Yes, I would have to say they do.'

I leant back, sated with my victory.

In heaven, no doubt, a thousand angels rejoiced in his.

To me, it looked like he had lost. To others around me, I suspect it looked like that too. Today I would agree with him. Today I admire him for his courage and his conviction. For being more concerned about the truth than winning a debating point or two.

I still remember that incident vividly. I don't know

his name. I've never seen him since. God used him.

Sometimes it looks like we lose. It looks like we lose in public. It looks like we are fools. Sometimes looks deceive.

One sows, another waters, another reaps.

Evangelism isn't just about decisions. It isn't just about giving someone the opportunity to make a decision for Christ. It's about being involved in the process of bringing someone along on the road from negativity or indifference to a positive decision for Christ. So we need to have confidence in God, that he is in fact working in us and through us in the process of bringing others to him.

## A WASTED HOLIDAY?

Katriina was a nurse, and had studied and worked with Renata for two years. Katriina was a Christian, Renata wasn't. The local Christian fellowship had planned a one-week skiing trip, and Katriina felt strongly she was meant to ask Renata along. One week before the trip, Katriina pulled some ligaments in her left leg and it was put in a cast. Not exactly the ideal physical condition for downhill skiing. Katriina decided not to go. Renata didn't want to go without her.

Katriina prayed about the issue. She decided to go on the trip, to take the time and invest the money, even though she herself would spend most of her time with her leg resting on a stool inside a chalet, listening to stories of how good the snow was and how exhilarating that turn by the trees was and how wonderfully tired everybody felt. But she was convinced it was important for Renata to go.

That weekend Renata became a Christian.

Katriina didn't lead her to Christ herself, but it was Katriina who obeyed God and who sacrificed time and money to ensure that Renata heard the gospel that week. God used her in the process.

## GOSPEL PERSPECTIVES ON GENERAL ISSUES

Evangelism is a process. And the reality that the Bible is relevant to every area of life can be demonstrated in conversations on almost any topic even if no biblical text is mentioned.

If you're a television watcher, you can chat to people about the storylines in your favourite soaps and the particular issues they are exploring at the time – AIDS, homosexuality, adultery. What should Sally do when she discovers Kevin is having an affair? Are homosexual relationships OK, as *EastEnders* argues so persuasively?

Sometimes the news provides a clear opportunity for discussion. In 1993 Britain was rocked by the brutal murder of a two-year-old boy, James Bulger, by two ten-year-olds. The details that emerged from the trial day by day transfixed the nation. It seemed to many that our society had reached a new depth of darkness. How could such a thing happen in 90s Britain? Press commentators seemed bewildered or forced into concluding, as one newspaper headline did, that James's murderers were 'freaks of nature'.

Here, in this tragic event, was an opportunity to discuss what the Bible has to say about the nature of human beings. Here, in this tragic event, was an opportunity to ask what future there might be for the two ten-year-old murderers if they don't experience forgiveness. Here, in this tragedy for James's parents and family, was an opportunity to ask what future there is for them if they cannot forgive the ghastly crime committed against their little son. In short, as Britain reeled at the daily bad news from the courtroom, there were probably millions of opportunities in canteens and bus queues, over coffee or lunch, to talk about the nature of humanity and the Good News of Jesus.

## GOSPEL PERSPECTIVES ON PERSONAL ISSUES

The Bible has something to say on virtually every issue in life that people face. And the people you work with are facing issues. Research suggests, for example, that many people in London are beset by a sense of purposelessness in their lives. On the surface life may be fine, but underneath, as one UK Billy Graham advertising campaign put it, 'Who can make sense of it?'

Beyond a sense of purposelessness there may be anxiety about redundancy, bereavement perhaps, a recent divorce, whether to continue that affair, illness in the family. It's not our business to pry. It's not part of our job description to become the company agony aunt. But it may be part of our role as Christians to be the kind of person people can talk to about problems. The two most important things we need are an open ear and a tender heart.

'All the lonely people, where do they all come from?' sang the Beatles in 1966. The situation hasn't improved over the years. Indeed, loneliness is a chronic disease in our society. Many people are yearning just for someone to listen to them. If we listen carefully, then perhaps we will find the right word to say at the right time. Perhaps we will be able to bring a biblical perspective to bear on the issue.

Sometimes we will find ourselves totally out of our depth, inadequate for the task. In this I am much encouraged by the story Jesus tells in Luke 11. It's worth quoting in full:

> 'Suppose one of you has a friend, and he goes to him at midnight and says, "Friend, lend me three loaves of bread, because a friend of mine on a

journey has come to me, and I have nothing to set before him."

'Then the one inside answers, "Don't bother me. The door is already locked, and my children are with me in bed. I can't get up and give you anything." I tell you, though he will not get up and give him the bread because he is his friend, yet because of the man's boldness he will get up and give him as much as he needs.

'So I say to you: Ask and it will be given to you; seek and you will find; knock and the door will be opened to you. For everyone who asks receives; he who seeks finds; and to him who knocks, the door will be opened...'

The story isn't just about persistence in prayer. It also makes the point that if I bring my friend to God in prayer, God will answer. *I* don't have the resources, but God does. And he will respond. What an encouragement!

## GOSPEL PERSPECTIVES ON BUSINESS ISSUES

The Bible has something to say about how we do the work we do. As Christians we need to work out not just what it means to be a Christian in accountancy, but what it means to be a Christian accountant. That is, how does my personal faith affect my public work? A Christian advertising executive, for example, will not only have to ask himself whether his ads are honest, decent, legal and truthful according to current social standards, but whether his ads are honest, decent, legal and truthful according to God's standards.

What perspectives on your work does the Bible bring to bear? On how to motivate people? On bringing up children? On how to sell? On being a mechanic? On Total Quality Management? If we want to change companies and industries for the better, we will have to wrestle with the issues they face and look for answers from the Bible. Making such an effort is really quite rare, and there is a deep need for people in similar jobs to get together to work through these issues. And a deep need for our ministers to help us. And a crying need for our theological colleges to train them to do so.

## GETTING THE MESSAGE OUT

Successful sports teams and successful businesses tend to have one thing in common – they know what they're there to do, which is to win games or to make products people will pay for. They know their objectives. But in our ministries it is easy to forget our overall objectives. For example:

- To bring glory to God through our work.
- To help bring people to know Christ.
- To make disciples.

These may seem very obvious on paper, but they are not so obvious in practice. Day by day.

Apparently the most common mistake professional salespeople make is that they don't ask for the sale. And perhaps one of the most common mistakes Christians make is that they never ask their friends or co-workers if they would like to become followers of Jesus.

I had been in my job at Ogilvy and Mather for four years. In my first two and a half years, I probably shared my personal testimony over thirty times. I was involved in an early morning meeting with a non-Christian, and another one with two Christians. I developed a number of solid friendships which I still have today. I prayed and I gave away a lot of books.

Sounds pretty good, doesn't it?

In that time, however, no one at Ogilvy and Mather became a Christian.

After two and a half years, the total known number of Christians at Ogilvy was five. About 0.3% of the corporate population. An evangelistic need greater than the one million Bambara in the Ivory Coast, the three hundred and fifty thousand Dagomba in Ghana, the two million Acehnese in North Sumatra. In fact, an evangelistic need greater than almost every ethnic group on earth. Fortunately, only my company was paying for my missionary efforts.

In the nine months that followed, the ministry grew dramatically. Three separate quiet-time groups started meeting in the mornings. A man called Ted began a Bible study. A prayer-chain with ten people was set up. Three people were involved in a 14-week Bible study after work in someone's flat. An excited, recommitted Christian woman appeared and quietly started developing a ministry. And, in response to prayer for more workers, a mature Christian man emerged. And four people became Christians.

At the spiritual level God clearly intervened. Perhaps we too were reaping the fruit of three years work and prayer. We did pray. We not only prayed generally, we prayed for growth. For more Christians to come. For more workers to come. And they came.

And we did actually ask people the crucial question: do you want this? We communicate the gospel through our behaviour, but at some point people need to hear the word. People need information to make a decision for Christ. In the nine fruitful months, I gave away ten copies of the longish gospel tract 'The Four Spiritual Laws' (now renamed 'Knowing God Personally') and I went through the material with three people. All three became Christians.

We must give people the information they need to make a decision. And ask them if they want to decide for Christ. This has nothing to do with high-pressure

Edge without guilt • 75

guilt manipulation. It is simply taking the initiative to ask them what is, after all, a natural and vital question: do you want Jesus in your life?

So from time to time it's good to consciously remind ourselves of why we are at work and to ask ourselves what fruit we have seen. Has anyone come to Christ? Have we seen any change in attitudes? Have we been able to develop relationships with anyone? Have we had an opportunity to share the gospel with anyone? Is there another Christian co-worker we could pray with? Have we been praying for opportunities for growth?

The problem for many of us is that we will do almost anything rather than directly share the gospel and ask someone if they are interested. I used to get quite tense as I got to that point in a conversation and often had to force myself forward, even though there was nothing in the other person's behaviour to indicate that they didn't want me to go on. Certainly there may be some kind of spiritual warfare when we get close to sharing the gospel with someone: it is, after all, not in Satan's best interests to see Christ's kingdom growing in citizens. Sometimes we put our reticence down to Britishness: we are not pushy. Or we call it sensitivity, when sometimes it's just plain cowardice. But the irony is that very often people *want* us to tell them about Jesus.

## HOLY BOLDNESS

Still, we need to recognise that it does take courage to share the Good News. This particular brand of courage is precisely the kind the Holy Spirit is in the habit of providing. In the book of Acts, two characteristics keep recurring in the description of the early disciples – joy and boldness. Often when they speak out, Luke records that they do so with boldness. Here's the response of the Sanhedrin after hearing Peter's speech in Acts 4 (my italics):

When they saw the *courage* of Peter and John and
realised that they were unschooled, ordinary
men, they were astonished and they took note
that these men had been with Jesus.

*Acts 4:13*

In Acts 4:29 Peter prays:

Now, Lord, consider their threats and enable your
servants to speak your word with great *boldness*.

In verse 31 it says that the prayer was answered:

And they were all filled with the Holy Spirit and
spoke the word of God *boldly*.

Look too at Acts 9:27–29; 13:46; 14:3; 18:24–26; 19:8.
This kind of boldness is not self-confidence nor the
product of an extrovert personality type but of the
Holy Spirit. God isn't asking us to change our person-
alities. He is asking us to make ourselves open to his
Spirit. Boldness can be gentle. Boldness can come with
a winsome smile. But it is unlikely to be silent. And
only the Spirit can give it to us.

## READY, STEADY, TONGUE-TIED?

One common barrier to telling people about the gospel
is not feeling confident you can explain it in simple, jar-
gon-free language that is understandable to someone
who has never set foot in a church. This is probably a
common problem.

First, it's worth saying that it is better to struggle to
communicate the truth about Jesus than not to try to
communicate it at all. Second, witnessing doesn't have
to be in the form of a prepared lecture – it can be just
like a conversation between two people.

On one occasion I was having a meal in a coffee
shop, and as I left I said to the waitress, 'I don't know

if you're interested but this is something about Jesus, that you might find interesting', offering her a little booklet. (It wasn't a great speech. Notice the repetition of 'interest' in two different forms.) But anyway, she replied, 'Oh yes, I belong to him.'

She witnessed simply, concisely, powerfully, communicating something rich about her relationship with Jesus. She belonged to him. She was his. And she was happy about it. The words spoke of Jesus' Lordship. The matter-of-fact way she said them spoke of her trust in him and her love for him.

That's witnessing at its simplest. But the Bible encourages us to be ready to give an account of what we believe, so it's worth thinking through how we might communicate the gospel to a non-Christian co-worker. There are a number of little booklets that set out various simple ways of communicating the gospel, and you can practice on someone in your housegroup. Another helpful tool is to be able to tell someone how you became a Christian – again using non-technical language to do so. Don't worry if you don't have a spectacular 'drugs-to-sainthood' testimony. What will interest the non-Christian is that it is *your* story and that Christ is real to you.

Witnessing in the workplace is done in word and deed, with respect for the truth and compassion for the listener.

It is hard. It seems to go against our British reserve to talk about anything as personal as religion. There was a time when there were three things the British didn't talk about over dinner – sex, politics and religion. Now there are only two – religion and death. So it can feel awkward.

At its best, witnessing is the natural overflowing of our relationship with Jesus. We don't have to be perfect to share Jesus. We don't have to be the best at our job to share Jesus. But we do – as one Christian organisation expresses it – have to 'take the initiative to share the gospel in the power of the Spirit and leave the results to God'.

As the kids' chorus goes, 'Be bold, be strong, for the Lord your God is with you.'

Ain't it the truth.

• • •

# • EPILOGUE •
## 'All that glitters…'

It had been a great conversation. I had felt free to talk to her at some length about Christ. She seemed attentive, interested, open. I was quite excited about what might happen next. It was Friday and she was going away for the weekend.

Come Tuesday there it was. I could hardly believe my eyes. There, on a piece of paper stuck to her bookshelf for all to see, were these words: 'He's alive, he's alive, he's alive'.

I said nothing. I didn't want to come across as over-eager or perhaps put her in a situation she wasn't ready for. But inside I was rejoicing. Imagine that. 'He's alive, he's alive, he's alive.' The good news of the resurrection writ large in an advertising executive's office! Hallelujah!

A couple of months later I discovered that one of her friends had sent her the piece of paper, and it referred not to Jesus but to another reputed sighting of the long dead king of rock 'n' roll, Elvis Presley.

Things ain't always what they seem. But even though the conversation I'd had with her had not lead at that time to a heartfelt conviction about Christ's resurrection, it was from another point of view a successful piece of witnessing. I'd taken 'the initiative to share the Good News in the power of the Spirit'. The results, as always, are up to God.

• • •

# • 6 •

# GETTING GOING

## or
## The twenty-minute start-up programme

*Procrastination, they say, is the thief of time.*
*And it doesn't do much for evangelism either.*

## VERSE AND MORE

Christina loved literature, so I gave her a copy of a seventeenth-century poem called 'Love' by one of the great English poets. It's one of my very favourite poems. It's about Jesus as creator, forgiver, love, encourager:

> Love bade me welcome; yet my soul drew back,
>     Guilty of dust and sin
> But quick-ey'd Love, observing me grow slack
>     From my first entrance in,
> Drew nearer to me, sweetly questioning,
>     If I lacked anything. .

> 'A guest,' I answer'd, 'worthy to be here':
>     Love said, 'You shall be he.'

'I, the unkind, the ungrateful? Ah, my dear
    I cannot look on thee.'
Love took my hand and smiling did reply,
    'Who made the eyes but I?'

'Truth, Lord, but I have marr'd them; let my shame
    Go where it doth deserve.'
'And know you not,' says Love, 'Who bore the
                                        blame?'

    'My dear, then I will serve.'
'You must sit down,' says Love, 'and taste my
                                        meat.'

    So I did sit and eat.

*George Herbert*

She read it and loved it.

Just before she went on holiday we had lunch and I offered her a selection of four(!) books for her summer reading, from the heavily spiritual to the entertaining. She took one or two. But I think I overdid it that time.

When we know people's interests, we can find ways to expose them to the truth that they may well enjoy. Whether it be a seventeenth-century verse, or something less highbrow and more contemporary like Steve Turner's poetry or rock music or...?

But do we know our co-workers that well?

## DEVELOPING A MINISTRY PLAN

At the beginning of chapter four I suggested you write down the names of three people in your workplace that you think God might particularly want you to relate to on a spiritual level. Now is the time to apply the principles we have looked at about developing relationships. Why not pray now and work through the questions below for one of your three people? (Don't worry too much if you don't know the answers to any of the questions. You don't need to know all these things to develop a relationship, but some of the answers might indicate where you could start.)

• • •

## Stage 1

*General questions:*
What kind of person is he?
What are his chief characteristics?
What are his hobbies, main interests?
What do you have in common with him?
What do you find difficult to accept about him?

*Questions about values and attitudes to God:*
What do you think is most important to him?
How do you think he views God?
What do you think he thinks of Christianity?
What do you think he thinks of Christians?
What does he think of you?
What barriers do you feel there might be to his becoming a Christian?
What areas in his life (if any) do you think he feels are most in need of change?
What attitudes, beliefs, misconceptions does he need to change?

## Stage 2

What specific things could you do to serve, help and encourage this person? In general? In his spiritual development?

• • •

The questions so far may have indicated that you actually know very little about the person. Or they may have shown you that there are specific areas of life that the person is concerned about – a teenage son, being single, a sense of purposelessness, whatever. In turn, this information might give you more specific ideas for:

- Prayer.

- Changing your attitude or behaviour towards that person.

- Reading, so as to be able to address issues from a Christian point of view.

- Asking other Christians for advice about particular issues.

- Giving or lending a book or article.

- Inviting the person to a particular kind of event.

- Introducing him to Christian friends with similar interests.

• • •

### Stage 3

What do you want to happen next?

### Stage 4

What steps are you going to take...

In the next week?
In the next month?
Within three months?

• • •

Obviously, it's important to pray about each of these steps and to be open to the Holy Spirit as you move forward. There's no particular reason why the Lord shouldn't give you a clear opportunity to share the gospel verbally with someone you really don't know that well. On the other hand, it may be that you know someone very well, but you feel the next step is simply to watch and pray. As Hamlet said, 'the readiness is all.'

• • •

### Stage 5

Share your plan with someone else who is prepared to support you in prayer.

### Stage 6

Come back to your answers in a month's time and evaluate:

What happened
What you learned
What you did
What you have seen God doing

• • •

May the Lord give you wisdom and boldness as you seek to know and do his will.

# THE BODY BUSINESS

### or
### The loneliness of the long-distance working Christian and how to conquer it

*The lone wolf dines alone.*
*And less often!*

*Though one may be overpowered, two can defend them-*
*selves. A cord of three strands is not quickly broken.*

Ecclesiastes 4:12

*Each one should use whatever gift he has received to*
*serve others, faithfully administering God's grace in*
*its various forms.*

1 Peter 4:10

Christianity is a body business. It's not about glorious individuals storming the strongholds of atheism, apathy and indifference like superspiritual Rambos. It's about the body of Christ working together. It's about supporting one another wherever God calls us as individuals. It's about putting our gifts at the service of one another so that the whole body grows.

Praying for one another. Training one another. Working through ethical issues together. Doing things for one another. Perhaps something highly practical and not obviously spiritual. Like doing someone's ironing because she has an opportunity to talk to a co-worker about Christ and needs some stuff ready for the morning. Or preparing the meal for the evangelistic Bible study that someone else is going to lead in someone else's house.

## INVOLVING CHRISTIANS OUTSIDE YOUR WORKPLACE

> When it comes to my role as a Christian at
> work, I feel unsupported by my fellowship.
>
> *Wendy Somerville, hospital consultant*

Wendy isn't alone in that feeling. Many Christians feel exactly the same way. But Wendy is rare in actually expressing such a feeling. Many Christians don't expect there to be any interest in the spiritual dimensions of their work, or their fellowship to support them in prayer. Except in times of crisis. The workplace and the people in it are not perceived as particularly significant, although much prayer will go into a leaflet campaign to invite people we don't know to a seeker service in the church. And appropriately so.

This lack of corporate prayer for the workplace suggests that we may have accepted the division our secular colleagues have drawn between the public world of nine to five, where our faith and our God are not meant to trespass, and the private world of five to nine where we can do what we like. Ultimately this lack of corporate prayer stems from the priorities of our leaders who have also been caught in the public/private divide. This stems from a false view of who the minister really is.

## WHO IS THE MINISTER?

In his letter to the Christians at Ephesus, Paul writes:

> It was he who gave some to be apostles, some to
> be prophets, some to be evangelists, and some to
> be pastors and teachers, to prepare God's people
> for works of service, so that the body of Christ
> may be built up...'
>
> *Ephesians 4:11–12*

So what, according to Paul, is the job of a pastor and

teacher? To equip the people of God for their ministry. The job of a pastor/teacher is primarily to be a coach – to resource *us* for *our* ministry, not just to equip us to be volunteers in theirs.

Of course, then we are in danger of saying, 'Well, pastors don't know what it's like. They don't go to work. They don't understand the challenges we face.'

This is a bogus argument.

Your pastor may also not have been involved in a serious car accident, committed adultery, faced death, been attracted to someone of the same sex, taken Ecstasy, lost a child/parent. But we don't say to ourselves, 'I won't go and talk to my pastor, because he won't understand – he hasn't been through it.'

Tell your pastor. Ask questions. Put your issues on his agenda. He has been trained to listen, trained to look into God's all-sufficient word and to come back with answers to the tough questions.

However, let's ask ourselves: even at a basic level, couldn't our church leaders teach us something about work and vocation, ambition and promotion? About handling the disappointment of being passed over? About success and failure? About our attitude to our bosses, honesty and truth-telling? About leisure?

Couldn't they teach us about Esther and Daniel, Joseph and Naaman's servant-girl, Lydia and Paul? Can't they visit us in our workplaces, and preach about working on Sunday? Perhaps update a harvest festival service to reflect the way people bring in their harvest in today's world? Include a three-minute 'missionary-at-work' slot in a service once a month?

Obviously they can, but we too need to have the right attitude to what church is about.

## WHEN IS THE CHURCH NOT THE CHURCH?

We believe that we are church when we are gathered together in a building. That we are church when we are in the neighbourhood. However, it is my impression that we don't believe we are still church when we are out there, scattered like so many grains of salt in the world.

But of course we are. It's like saying that I am married to my wife, Katriina, when I am at home, but not when I am at work. She is meant to be interested in me, to support me and pray for me in all my responsibilities as a husband and father at home. But when I step out the door to got to work? Well, then I'm on my own.

The church is always the church. When we are gathered together, showing people by the way we love one another that we are Jesus' disciples (John 13:35). And when we are scattered like salt to work out our faithfulness to Christ in the world at large. So we shouldn't go to work alone. We should go to work with all the resources of God's work and God's people and God's Spirit. Do we?

Wendy, I am glad but somewhat ashamed to confess, is in my housegroup. She hadn't felt supported in her work by our group, though I think she would have felt supported in other areas of her life. Certainly, we had prayed for some specific situations – relationships and patient care and the restructuring of the Health Service – but actually we had only the sketchiest notion of what she did day by day, who she worked with, what kind of pressures she was under, what kind of issues she faced. So, one evening we asked her to give us a sketch of a day in her life. It took an hour. Some people's jobs are less complex and might only have taken ten minutes. But at the end of the time we had a much clearer picture of how Wendy spends 65% of her life, and therefore how we can pray for her.

But as a group we're not there yet. Because we're still not asking the spiritual questions about work automatically. Nor seeking prayer from one another for work issues automatically. Nor challenging one another about ministry in our workplaces or wherever it is that God has put us. We need to re-orient our thinking – not to make work issues the primary issues or even the dominant issues, but rather to redress the balance so that people know that God and God's people are genuinely interested in the way they spend 65% of their waking lives.

Stephen Pacht works in Paris. He used to be an accountant. Now he's working for Jews For Jesus. I see him maybe four times a year – quite a lot really for an overseas missionary. He sends me his prayer-letters, and there are usually requests to pray for people by name. People I will probably never meet this side of heaven.

By contrast, Wendy, Kevin, David, Pat and Claire are all members of my housegroup. I see them most Tuesday evenings and four times a month at church. But I don't know the name of one person that any of them works with. And I don't think we have ever prayed for the salvation of any of their colleagues. *They* probably have, but as a group we haven't. Why?

Maybe because Stephen is a missionary. And Wendy, Kevin, David, Pat and Claire are not. Or so we think.

But who meets more non-Christians in a day? Who spends more time with them? Who do non-Christians see struggling with anger and frustration, success and failure, limited resources and sexual temptation, gossip and the challenge to tell the truth, the threat and sometimes the reality of redundancy?

Wendy in the maelstrom of the National Health Service? Or Stephen over lunch in a Paris bistro?

In sum, where is someone more likely to see the

difference Jesus makes to a life? In Wendy's situation or Stephen's?

So why are so many of our evangelistic initiatives – and good initiatives they are – centred around local neighbourhoods and getting people into the church building to hear the minister, rather than about helping us to minister where we are?

Who should we pray for? Stephen or Wendy?

Certainly for the Stephens of the world. The whole world needs to hear the Good News.

But what about the Wendys? Why are we more inclined to pray for missionaries overseas or our ministers than for them?

How can you encourage other Christians in their ministry at work, wherever it might be? If you are in a housegroup, this might be the perfect context. You see one another regularly enough to share what's going on and to encourage one another in performance, relationships and witness.

Perhaps you might begin by having a regular ten-minute slot focused on work for five or six weeks. After that, people may well have become sufficiently conscious of work issues for these to be a more natural part of what they share and what they ask others about. Or you might have a prayer-partner you could share with. Or if you are married, you might make a point of praying for one another's workplaces, making them both matters for mutual concern. Even, and perhaps especially, if one of them is actually the home.

Or you could fill in 'The M File' at the end of this chapter and give everyone a copy, or pin it up on the missionary noticeboard in your church. Just imagine that you're a missionary (you are, aren't you?) and that your workplace is your mission field, and answer the questions accordingly.

## INVOLVING CHRISTIANS IN YOUR WORKPLACE

There may well be other Christians in your workplace. If there are, you and they may find it very helpful to meet regularly to pray or talk through issues that you face in your work. Pray that God will lead you to them.

My first meetings were with a Roman Catholic guy, and we read the psalms together. Later I met mainly with non-Christians on a one-to-one basis. Then a number of Christians came to the firm, and we began to meet weekly for prayer. That fizzled out after a bit, but then for a long time I met with another Roman Catholic man who had evangelism and encouragement very much on his heart. He kept me going. And he kept us praying. Then I nervously asked the managing director to allow us to use a conference room for a monthly lunchtime meeting. He agreed, and often a dozen or more attended, with twenty-five or thirty people on the 'mailing' list. After a couple of years that fizzled out.

Try things. Start things. Persevere. But feel free to stop things when they're not working for anyone.

Some people use the company noticeboard to advertise meetings. A friend of mine, who had been in his current job just nine months, did so and is now one of a group of five who meet weekly. It is encouraging for all the Christians there, and it may well provide a safe first-stop for someone who is mildly interested in Jesus but wouldn't set foot in a church for all the Guinness in Ireland.

Still, it takes courage to pin your name next to Jesus' on the company noticeboard. The moment you do you will probably feel somewhat vulnerable and start to think that everyone is looking at you strangely.

You may well be right.

# THE M-FILE
## Getting the truth out there

Name: ..................................................................

Occupation: .........................................................

Location of main mission activity: ...........................
..............................................................................

Number of people in my main area of activity (eg work, neighbourhood, club) ...............................................

Number of people I have contact with in a week:
..............................................................................

Number of Christians among my weekly contacts:
..............................................................................

What has happened in the mission over the last three months:

..............................................................................
..............................................................................
..............................................................................
..............................................................................

Who is praying for the mission:

..............................................................................
..............................................................................
..............................................................................

Main challenges I face:

..............................................................................
..............................................................................
..............................................................................
..............................................................................

What I would like prayer for:

..............................................................................
..............................................................................
..............................................................................

# • 8 •

# ROMEO/JULIET

### or
### Love's labours won

*The path to hell may be paved with good intentions,
but the path to heaven is certainly strewn with mixed
motives.*

## • CASE STUDY •
### Romeo/Juliet

Romeo/Juliet is whichever sex you are not.

Twenty-seven years old. Pretty cute. University educated and smart. Says what he/she likes in a forthright but not unkind or aggressive manner. Nevertheless, can be a bit intimidating. Comes from a Protestant background, but is not a churchgoer. Has a significant other who is pretty significant – been going out a couple of years. Not engaged. Has quite a few friends, some fairly long-standing. Likes movies, runs a literature group. Goes to the health club, likes to dance. Good at the job. Well-liked. Family lives in Surbiton.

How would you go about witnessing to this individual? What particular challenges do you think you might face?

• • •

## WHAT HAPPENED

'Juliet' worked for me. Her name was Jill. I was single. I fell in love. There were at least three barriers to saying anything about it to her:

1 She worked for me.
2 She wasn't a Christian.
3 She had a boyfriend.

I prayed a lot for her. Every day for months. All kinds of prayers, all kinds of verses, telling myself and God that his will would be best. At one stage I persuaded myself, by a convoluted piece of fanciful scriptural interpretation, that God might be saying Jill was the one for me. I asked God to show me one way or another within six months. I'm not sure I'd give God those kind of deadlines now, but I was young and in love. It was 21 February.

Then Jill stopped working for me.

One down.

Then she became a Christian.

Two down.

She hadn't left her boyfriend. But on 17 August, in a gush of Elizabethan rhetoric, I told her how I felt about her.

On 21 August, six months to the day, Jill told me she had split up with her boyfriend. Three down.

She also told me, kindly but in no uncertain terms, that there was no way we were going to become an item. God had answered my prayer. I couldn't pretend to be grateful.

Four down.

Of course, I didn't believe her. But she was right. I didn't turn out to be her Romeo. Nor she my Juliet.

The nuts and bolts of how she became a believer illustrate some important points about witness at work:

- There was **exposure to a Christian**. However flawed I was, however selfishly motivated, I was there.

  And it turned out that I was the right person for Jill. She had had a very negative view of Christians – stupid and no fun. Apparently I was neither. Every Monday she used to ask me if I'd had a good weekend, and I would reply, 'Yes.' After a while this began to get to her. The issue here is not that I have an upbeat, happy-go-lucky, sometimes infuriatingly jolly, noisy and childish personality. The issue is that God put Jill in contact with the right person for her.

  But I didn't know at the time she had a negative view of Christians – I was just there. So indeed it may well be that you, whatever your personality type and gifts, are just the right person for someone, or for quite a lot of the people, you work with right now. And you probably won't know that till afterwards.

- There was **prayer**. However mixed my motives. I was at least trying to pray for her salvation and growth with no rings attached.

- There was the development of **a relationship**, discussions about all sorts of things, eventually including spiritual matters. She heard the word. That involved me in some risk. I had to tell her at some point that I was a Christian. What would she think?

So faith comes from what is heard, and what is heard comes through the word of Christ.

*Romans 10:17, NRSV*

- There was **exposure to the scriptures**. I invited her to read the Bible with me one morning a week before work for ten or fifteen minutes. She agreed. She read the word for herself.

- One day I **shared the gospel** with her using a simple gospel plan. I challenged her. There was risk involved there too. In fact, I thought she accepted the Lord that day. Later, though, she told me it wasn't a genuine moment of commitment.

- I invited her to a five-week evangelistic Bible study with several other people. Further exposure to the word. More risk on my part. She was, after all, my subordinate, and I certainly didn't want her to feel in any way that I was using my position to pressure her – a kind of evangelistic harassment. The study was subsequently extended for another six weeks or so, and I involved Sandy, a mature Christian woman of about Jill's age. There was the **witness of other Christians**.

  After that study ended, Sandy invited her and the other women in the group to a study. Jill agreed to go.

All this over about a fifteen-month period. God using exactly those tools that Jim Petersen points to in his book, *Evangelism as a Lifestyle*:

1 The witness of the individual.
2 The witness of the word.
3 The witness of other Christians – the body.
4 The witness of the Spirit drawing Jill to himself.

And a fifth – God's sovereign control over events.

At one point Jill started to read Matthew's Gospel on her own and skip around churches a bit. But wherever she went there was a sermon on Matthew waiting just for her. After a while this began to get to her. Someone up there was trying to tell her something.

You may think you are alone in seeking to win someone to the Lord, but there is a whole army of other Christians out there who God might use. And all the ingenuity of his creative mind and his awesome Spirit. Even if you are alone, one plus God – as Elijah demonstrated so clearly in his confrontation with the prophets of Baal and Asherah (1 Kings 18) – is a distinct majority.

> 'Not by might nor by power, but by my Spirit,'
> says the Lord Almighty.
>
> *Zechariah 4:6*

Finally, this case illustrates something very important.

Evangelism is not an event. It is not just something that happens when the Good News is shared and Christ invites someone into his kingdom.

Evangelism is not an event. It is a process. The Spirit moving a person from where they are, through all kinds of means, towards their own encounter with Jesus. Jill became a Christian. So did our boss David. God used us both. But most of the people we worked with, prayed for and witnessed to, haven't become Christians. Or at least not yet.

Evangelism is a process. Only God knows how he will use your witness, how your witness will contribute in the future. As Paul points out in his first letter to the Christians in Corinth:

> What, after all, is Apollos? And what is Paul? Only servants, through whom you came to believe – as the Lord has assigned to each his task. I planted the seed, Apollos watered it, but God made it grow. So neither he who plants nor he who waters is anything, but only God, who makes things grow.
>
> *I Corinthians 3:5–7*

Prayer, initiative, risk – and God at work.

# WORK IS A
# SEVEN-LETTER WORD

### or
### A whiff of excellence is worth
### a ton of mediocrity

*They didn't want it good.*
*They wanted it on Wednesday.*

Robert Heimleur

*Pastor C H Spurgeon once asked a young girl, who*
*served as a domestic in one of his families ... what evi-*
*dence she could give of having become a Christian, and*
*she meekly answered, 'I now sweep under the mats.'*

The Family Friend, 1885, S W Partridge & Co

## • SNAPSHOT •
## The accidental birth of a hero

When I was about eighteen, I went to spend nine months
working on a kibbutz. I was looking forward to the outdoor
life, the sunshine on my face, the soil beneath my feet and
the fruit trees all around.

My first job was doing the dishes.

Inside.

The electric light on my face. The tiles beneath my feet.
And the walls all around.

About an hour or so into the job someone brought over
a huge stainless-steel ovenrack. It probably had twenty
shelves on it. 'Give that a clean will you.'

It was filthy. It looked to me as if it hadn't been cleaned

properly in about a decade. Encrusted with goo, hardened by a million hours in the oven at high temperatures, its essential colour was not gleaming silver but browny-black. Resentfully, I began to clean it.

After a while I realised it was going to take me a couple of hours. My resentment began to build. I felt that these kibbutzniks were taking advantage of this new foreigner, giving me a job no one else had been bothered to do for weeks.

Maybe months. Maybe years.

Maybe since the day it was bought.

After about an hour and a half I was getting really angry. But I carried on. There didn't seem much choice.

'Wow,' said the person who gave me the job, as she saw how the stainless steel had emerged from fifteen or so of the racks, 'I only meant give it a quick wipe.'

The word went round the kibbutz that I was an outstanding worker. Rather like the glorious Charge of the Light Brigade, it was just a terrible misunderstanding.

But I never told them that.

• • •

## THE PURSUIT OF EXCELLENCE

Billy Graham's wife probably has a different attitude. I have never been to her house, but the story goes that she has a plaque above her kitchen sink which reads: 'Divine services conducted here three times daily.'

Work is ordained by God. And it should be dedicated to God. As we saw earlier, the Hebrew word for work is *avodah*, the same as the word for worship. 'Service' captures the flavour best. Work is a seven-letter word – service – to God and people. And though I would lose my job if I built a theology on the basis of that observation alone, we can see elsewhere in scripture that work is part of the 'everything' we do 'to the glory of God'. For God, work is part of our worship. It is part of our service to him. We submit our work not just to our earthly boss but to our heavenly boss, God. Here is Paul writing to first-century slaves:

> Whatever you do, work at it with all your heart,
> as working for the Lord, not for men...
>
> *Colossians 3:23*

God could hardly expect us to work 'with all our heart' unless the work itself was of some significance to him. Some tasks may not seem very important to the people in your organisation, but they are important to God. Work isn't just a platform for evangelism and ministry. It is significant in itself. This is why quality is important.

How good is the work you do? Good enough to be offered to God? Pause a moment and think not of your job as a whole but of a specific task you do at work.

Now add the thought, 'I am doing this for God'.

Here are some examples:

- Changing a nappy that overfloweth – for God.

- Answering the phone for the twenty-third time in the last fifteen minutes – for God.

- Writing a report on the attitudes of Kansas City housewives, aged 35–49, towards decaffeinated coffee in general and Maxwell House decaffeinated in particular – for God.

- Going to lunch with a difficult and slightly unpleasant client who you would rather not see this side of the 4th millenium – for God.

## CAUTION – ATHEIST AT WORK

This call to good work I call the Nimrod Principle. Here's what Genesis 10:8–9 has to say:

> Nimrod ... grew to be a mighty warrior on the
> earth. He was a mighty hunter before the Lord;
> that is why it is said, 'Like Nimrod, a mighty
> hunter before the Lord.'

Two things strike me here. First, Nimrod was only a
hunter, but he gets his name into God's book because
he was a 'mighty hunter'. Second, he did his hunting
'before the Lord'. In some way he felt himself accountable to God for the way he did his work. Think for a
moment of your job and add the phrase 'before the
Lord.'

Bryan – a mighty plumber – before the Lord.

Sarah – a mighty electrician – before the Lord.

Suppose for a moment you are wordprocessing a letter and you know it is going to be sent to the Queen.
You probably read it sixteen times before you print it
out. And you print it out on the best paper you have.
Then you think, 'Well, maybe if I just changed that
word, it might perhaps read slightly better.' So you
change it. Read it sixteen times. And print it out again.
And check it again.

How carefully we do our work is often determined
by who we think is going to see it. Maybe the letter is
not for the Queen or even the president of the company,
but that shouldn't make any difference.

Most of us are atheists when it comes to our work.
We don't think God is looking.

## 'T' FOR...?

One thing I've tried from time to time is to choose one
job on my 'To do' list and dedicate it specifically to
God, marking it with the letter 'T' for task. It changes
my attitude to that particular task and also to the other
tasks on the list. That 'T' winks at me from the list – a
little reminder of the appropriate perspective for all my

tasks. If only I used the 'T' every day.

God is interested in excellence in everything we do. Joseph, Nehemiah and Daniel are three obvious examples of career success combined with outstanding service to God in a pagan environment. God seeks excellence and he rewards it. When he is looking for a craftsman to make the ark, the tent of meeting and its furnishings, he tells Moses the particular individual he wants for the job – Bezalel. And he makes it quite clear which Bezalel he means – 'son of Uri, the son of Hur, of the tribe of Judah'. A man filled with his Spirit and 'with skill, ability and knowledge in all kinds of crafts' (Exod 31:2–3).

Similarly, when Solomon needs someone to do the bronzework in the temple, no one within his own borders is good enough. He has Hiram, a man of mixed Israelite/Tyrian blood brought down from Tyre. Only the best will do.

## LITTLE BIG THINGS

*In Search of Excellence* was one of the best-selling management books of the 80s. Here's a quote from the introduction:

> For us, one of the main clues to corporate excellence has come to be just such incidents of unusual effort on the part of apparently ordinary individual employees.
>
> *Peters and Waterman, HarperCollins, p XVII.*

Great companies are made great not by stand-out individuals producing extraordinary work, but by ordinary people going the extra mile, striving to do the basic things really well.

I was in the supermarket the other day. When I got to the checkout, the young man waiting there looked at me and said, 'Good afternoon, sir', and smiled.

'Good afternoon,' I replied, already registering surprise. Normally I have to initiate any greeting with checkout people. He was fast, efficient, slightly formal.

'How would you like to pay, sir?'

No one ever calls me 'Sir'. Maybe I'm just getting old. But actually I liked it in his case – it was a mark of respect to a customer and it wasn't said coldly.

'Would you sign here?'

'Thank you.'

'Goodbye.'

Everything about the encounter was efficient, helpful and respectful. It was also unusual. Maybe doing the checkout is boring and I don't know how he was feeling. But I felt that I was an important and valued human being as I left the store with my milk and apples.

This kind of service is unusual. Some companies really do go for excellence. But you might just as easily find yourself in a job where standards are quite low and morale poor. In such a situation, our standards remain God's, not our boss's or the company's. And, in fact, excellence can be infectious. Even a little bit of it. When one person starts doing things really well, it tends to generate two kinds of response – either resentment or a desire to do things equally well.

## AVOIDING THE GUILT TRAP

The call to excellent work, however, isn't intended to burden us with false guilt about not being the best at whatever it is we do. The Bible clearly recognises different levels of ability. Bezalel is a craftsman of a higher quality than Oholiab, the man God names as his number two. They, in turn, are presumably better than the other craftsmen whom God has, as he says, also given the ability to finish the work. Nevertheless, all are capable of work that is pleasing to God.

In the parable of the talents (Matt 25:14–30), one man is given two talents, another five. Both double their talents. Both make the most of what they have been given. God commends them both. Biblical success is making the most of what we have been given by God. It is not necessarily doing better than other people. This is an important distinction: we don't have to be the fastest bricklayer on the site, or in the town, or in the country, or in the world to please God.

## PERSONAL BEST?

Certainly, competition can be healthy. It can be a spur to improved performance. But competition can also be fuelled by envy, malice, greed, pride – a host of dark motivations that can embitter the individual, transform workplace relationships into a minefield of political intrigue, and turn company rivalries sour, even criminal, in the attempt to win.

Biblical success is not running faster than anyone else. It isn't just running the best time you can.

It's running the best time you can – with God's help.

We cannot do excellent work in an excellent way in our own strength. We can produce excellent work in our own strength, but not in a way that pleases God. Jesus is quite clear on this:

> 'I am the vine, you are the branches. Those who
> abide in me and I in them bear much fruit,
> because apart from me you can do nothing.'
>
> *John 15:5, NRSV*

Ultimately, Jesus is the equipper. And not just spiritually. David, the warrior king, records that it is God who trained his hands for war (Psalm 144:1). The writer to the Hebrews prays that Jesus, that great Shepherd of the sheep, might equip the Hebrews with everything good for doing God's will (Heb 13:20–21). It is through Christ that God equips us to do what is pleasing to him. As Le Roy Eims once said:

> The greatest way to maintain a spirit of excellence in our lives is an absolute yielding of our lives to the person of Jesus Christ himself.

## AN EXTRA MILE?

It isn't just that Jesus does all things well so that he becomes our example. It is also that he helps us to steer the course between two important and sometimes apparently conflicting ideas.

The first comes out of these words of Jesus:

> 'So you also, when you have done everything you were told to do, should say, "We are unworthy servants; we have only done our duty."'
>
> Luke 17:10

Is this not a call to go the extra mile? To do more than your job description requires, and go above and beyond the call of duty?

But what if our duty already requires sixty hours a week? Is there no end to the labour? And is that not in tension with Jesus' invitation:

> 'Come to me, all you who are weary and burdened, and I will give you rest. Take my yoke upon you and learn from me, for I am gentle and humble in heart, and you will find rest for your souls. For my yoke is easy and my burden is light.'
>
> Matthew 11:28–30

One of the ways to know how to respond to work demands is to go to Jesus. For many, excellence often has a devastatingly high price. It may only come with hard work, late nights, dinners slowly turning to powder in the oven and, in many cases, divorce. Work can become the great idol, and it is a voraciously hungry idol with an insatiable appetite for people's best time and best energies. If you are married, the excuse that 'it's all for the family' may soon wear thin unless the family have been involved in the decision to make those kinds of sacrifices. It probably doesn't have to be that way.

The key is not just to ask Jesus how you can be excellent in your job, but rather what kind of overall life will be most pleasing to God. The question is always: where does Jesus call you to follow him? And the answer he gives you, like the answer he gave to the apostle Peter and the apostle John, will be for you alone, and may be totally different from the answer he gives to the Christian at the next desk.

In tough times, go to Jesus.

Sandy did. She was organising a big corporate conference with senior executives flying in from all over the country. And travel plans and requirements in constant flux. She began to feel overwhelmed. That day God spoke to her in her quiet time. She was reading the story of the feeding of the five thousand. There seemed no way Jesus could feed all those people, but a young lad had five loaves and two fishes and made them available to Jesus. Jesus took what he brought and made it more than enough. On that day Sandy felt God was saying to her, 'Bring to me what you have and I will supply the rest.'

In tough times, when we are weary and strung out, we can only bring what we have to God and ask him to supply the rest.

## EXCELLENCE OPENS DOORS

'Do you see a man skilled in his work?
  He will serve before kings;
  he will not serve before obscure men.'

Proverbs 22:29

Nehemiah is a good example (Neh 1–2). He is cup-bearer to the most powerful human on the planet – Artaxerxes, the Persian emperor. Cupbearing was an important job, entrusted to a senior official. The cup-bearer was, after all, the last person to handle the wine before the emperor drank it. If you happened to be an emperor in the fifth century BC, you chose your cup-bearer very, very, very carefully. Artaxerxes had good reason to be wary – he had probably had to execute two of his brothers for rebellion.

Nehemiah had made it to this top position even though he wasn't a Persian but an exiled Israelite, a member of a defeated and dispersed nation. It was the emperor's trust of Nehemiah and his personal concern for him that opened the door for Nehemiah to ask for leave of absence and the resources to rebuild Jerusalem. And that concern was built on his job performance.

Our work is important to God in itself, but it is also important as a component of our witness to our co-workers. We are at work to work. We are expected to produce good work. Work of one kind or another is what we produce. And we are viewed by people around us in the context of our work. Good work commands respect. Poor work, shoddy work, late work make it much harder to develop respect and therefore the kind of open relationship in which the gospel can be communicated. Good work can be a platform for ministry and evangelism. But, quite apart from that, it is just down-right satisfying to do something as well as you can.

Even cleaning ovenracks.

# • 10 •

# WHO'S THE KING OF THE CASTLE?

## or
## Relating to your boss

*I don't want any yes men around me.*
*I want everybody to tell me the truth,*
*even if it costs them their jobs.*

Samuel Goldwyn

# • SNAPSHOT •
## Pride comes before a fight

It's party time.

Our whole group is going out to celebrate a couple of promotions, to say thanks to some people who are moving to a different part of the company, to celebrate the boss's fortieth birthday, to build team morale. It's a welcome breather after a gruelling couple of months.

I go to a local bakery and buy a birthday cake big enough to feed twenty-five, large and fluffy, and layered and peaked with cream. Later that evening we arrive at an elegant Italian restaurant, sip drinks, savour the antipasti, relish the main course. Good-natured banter bounces round the long table. We say well-done and thanks and – as the large, fluffy, cream-dream arrives – happy birthday. The cake is divided up, and more good-natured banter bounces round the long table.

Then my boss and the second-in-command, well-built sportsmen the pair, rise from their seats, a plate of fluffy, cream-topped cake in each hand. They come round the table and converge at my chair. They are standing over me. Good-naturedly, they threaten the worst. Good-naturedly, I do my best to feign a kind of Clint Eastwood cool. 'Go on,' I think to myself, 'make my day.'

Suddenly there's cake all over me.

I'm out of my seat so fast it makes Lynford Christie look like a snail in wellies. With a surge of angry adrenaline I have pushed my boss, the birthday boy, caught him off balance and sent him across the room crashing onto a table and then onto the floor, accompanied by a chair and some knives and forks. I am about to throw a punch at his second-in-command.

The Christian at work.

• • •

## WHO IS THE BOSS?

Our relationship with our boss is often the most difficult relationship we have at work. It may not necessarily feel that way. In fact, many Christians I have talked to feel that it's just fine. But as we have explored the issue further, God's word and Spirit have often uncovered resentments and rebellions that we were previously unaware of. These resentments may sometimes arise out of personality clashes or the perceived failings of the boss, or indeed from the tensions caused by our own inadequate performance. At root, however, the problem in relating to our boss often comes from two sources.

First, pride – the difficulty most of us have in willingly and wholeheartedly submitting to anyone's authority. Few of us like to give up our independence. Few of us like to be in a situation where someone can say 'Jump' and we have to. Most of us are in that situation.

Second, fear. At a time when millions of people are without paid work, our boss seems to wield even greater power. The power not only to deprive us of this job, but to send us out into a marketplace where it may prove extremely difficult to find another one.

Furthermore, our contemporary understanding of the biblical concepts of fatherhood and love may be rather more romantic and cuddly than originally intended. Certainly, the father in the Bible is there to protect, provide and nurture. But he is also there to be obeyed. Similarly, Jesus emphasises the strong connection between love and obedience:

> 'If you love me, you will obey what I command.'
>
> *John 14:15*

> 'Whoever has my commands and obeys them, he is the one who loves me.'
>
> *John 14:21*

Love is inextricably connected with submission to authority.

## PRIDE OF PLACE

On the whole, Western culture has a problem with authority. We respect the law less than we used to, we are suspicious of our politicians, we filter the media for moral and political bias, we accept our teachers' views more reluctantly than previous generations, we are more wary of the police than we used to be, and so on. Much of this suspicion is realistic and healthy. Authority is based on trust and if authority is abused then trust inevitably breaks down.

The dangers of misused authority are clear and writ large across the history of this and every preceding century. The Bible calls its leaders – whether political, religious, commercial or family – to use their God-given power in the service of others. Indeed, there is in the Bible a particular emphasis placed on the responsibility of the powerful to protect the powerless. The measure of the righteous king in the Old Testament is not how he treats his generals and landowners but how he treats the widow and the orphan and the alien – the vulnerable segments of the population. Similarly, the biblical legislation about employer/employee relations puts a heavy emphasis on justice and fair dealing.

It may not be our experience, but authority structures are intended for our benefit:

- **To help us grow in wisdom and character.** We can see this in the roles of parents, extended family, teachers and bosses. A good boss is a teacher – someone who helps us to develop skills, to anticipate and solve problems, to develop character traits that will help us do our job better, and to overcome those weaknesses that affect our performance and working relationships.

- **To help protect us from destructive temptations.** A good boss protects his people from themselves and from the poor decisions and behaviour that might affect the business and them badly.

- **To help us receive direction for decisions.** A good boss sets and clarifies the overall direction, sets priorities and is a sounding board for decisions. A good boss also ensures that his people have the resources to do the job.

This model of a good boss partially parallels the role of

God's authority in our lives. Obedience to God's authority is for our benefit.

In Eden, Adam failed to trust the truth of God's words and the reality of God's good intentions. God, he felt, was withholding something desirable from him and was protecting himself from having rivals. Adam failed to recognise his own limitations and thought he knew better. We all have our limitations. And we don't necessarily know best. We need to approach God, and indeed those set in authority above us, with humility. Again, they won't always be right – the world is full of corrupt companies and individuals – but our response to our boss shouldn't spring from self-centredness, self-righteousness or selfish ambition, but from a conscious awareness that his authority has been put into our lives for a benevolent purpose. And that purpose, like Joseph's unjust imprisonment by Potiphar (Gen 39:1–20), may not always be immediately apparent.

## FEAR OF FALLING

Many of us believe that:

- The boss has authority.
- The boss has our future in his/her hands.

But are these beliefs actually true?

First, a startling biblical example.

## TWO GREAT CAREER OPPORTUNITIES?

Saul is king. David is not. David has been remarkably successful in everything Saul has asked him to do, and Saul recognises that the Lord is with David and no longer with him. Saul sets out to try to thwart God's plan. As a result David, having already survived at least four assassination attempts, finds himself chased around Israel by Saul and his army.

On two occasions, at Engedi and again in Saul's field camp, David has a clear opportunity to kill Saul. Not unnaturally, David's men, who probably took no particular delight in being the objects of Saul's persistent and apparently vindictive pursuit, encourage him to do so. They see the opportunity as God-given.

But David refuses to kill the man in authority, nor will he allow anyone else to do his dirty work for him (1 Sam 26:9). This has nothing to do with Saul's *behaviour* but everything to do with Saul's *status before God*. Saul is the Lord's anointed. The man placed in authority by God. David, unlike Saul, understands that the king's authority comes from God. Saul wasn't anointed king because he was the finest warrior: he was made king because God chose him. However, Saul cannot trust in that anointing enough to obey God. David, by contrast, has already been anointed by Samuel to be the next king. But he won't hasten his own coronation by raising his hand against the Lord's anointed. David is determined to wait for God's timing and God's means of installing him on the throne.

## AUTHORITY FROM GOD

Saul's authority is from God. And David will flee from Saul, but he won't seek to usurp that authority, even though it is being so badly abused. Saul has authority – from God.

Another biblical example of submission to authority in action is Jesus before Pilate.

> 'Do you refuse to speak to me?' Pilate said. 'Don't you realise I have power either to free you or to crucify you?'
> Jesus answered, 'You would have no power over me if it were not given to you from above.'
>
> John 19:10–11

Jesus, the Son of God, has all power and authority, but he submits to Pilate because of the authority Pilate has been given by God.

Pilate is, in fact, misusing his authority. It's quite clear to him that Jesus is innocent of the charges against him. However, he allows himself to be manipulated by the Jewish leadership. Jesus' point isn't only that Pilate has received his authority from God and is accountable to him for its use, but also that he is prepared to submit to Pilate's abuse of that power because this is God's will for him at that time.

The question is, do our secular bosses gain their authority from God?

> Let every person be subject to the governing authorities; for there is no authority except from God, and those authorities that exist have been instituted by God. Therefore whoever resists authority resists what God has appointed, and those who resist will incur judgement.
>
> *Romans 13:1–2, NRSV*

Here Paul is writing to the Christians in Rome and talking specifically about civil authority, an authority that many scholars believe had already grown unjustly hostile towards Christians. Nevertheless, Paul says 'submit'. Importantly, he doesn't argue from the specific circumstances of the situation but from a general principle: 'For there is no authority except from God...'

Our boss's authority comes from God. That does not mean all her decisions do. Neither does it necessarily mean that Christians are never to be involved in overthrowing corrupt, tyrannical political regimes. A soldier is expected to obey a superior officer without question, but even within strict military discipline allowance is made for disobedience. It does mean, however, that unless some more important principle is being flouted, we are to obey our boss. There may be exceptions, but it is important in developing the right attitude to recognise the general principle: we obey our boss primarily because we thereby obey God. That is, we recognise that he has decreed there should be structures of authority as a means of bringing order and justice to human relations. This doesn't mean we are to obey unwise decisions without question. It does mean that we need to be careful before we challenge someone's authority.

In his letter to Titus Paul gives us another reason for obedience:

> Teach slaves to be subject to their masters in everything, to try to please them, not to talk back to them, and not to steal from them, but to show that they can be fully trusted, so that in every way they will make the teaching about God our Saviour attractive.
>
> *Titus 2:9–10*

Our behaviour is meant to make the gospel attractive to those in authority over us, and our submission to them is perhaps understandably the first thing Paul points to. If someone doubts our basic acceptance of their right to direct, then there really is no basis for a healthy working relationship.

## SILENCE IS GOLDEN...

Mike Z was a Christian financial controller. A friendly, outgoing man who took a job working for a Jewish millionaire in a successful small business. To get to his boss's office Mike had to pass through an open-plan office area. As he did so, he would say 'Hello' to those who noticed him going through. It seemed the natural, friendly thing to do. His boss told him that he didn't want him talking to anyone on the way to his office. This seemed entirely unreasonable and somewhat cold, and Mike continued to greet his co-workers.

His boss told him not to.

Mike prayed about the situation and decided to do what his boss told him rather than follow conventional working practice.

A while later, his boss came up to him and said, 'You're a born-again Christian, aren't you?' Mike nodded, wondering what was coming.

'Well,' his boss continued, 'I'm looking to hire some more people. Know any of your kind who might be interested?'

Mike's submission, as well as his general performance, had adorned the gospel. His employer wasn't yet a Christian, but he recognised the difference Christ made in someone's life. And, to him at least, its commercial value.

Submission to human authority clearly has its limits. There is no call in scripture to do things that are clearly immoral, illegal or against God's laws. The opposite is true. And this could cost a Christian his job. There is a need to look carefully at any problem situation and to discern whether there are solutions that meet the boss's agenda and that are, nevertheless, in line with God's laws. Daniel provides an excellent example.

## DIET RIGHT – A DIPLOMAT'S GUIDE

Daniel, a young Israelite of significant intellectual and administrative promise, finds himself selected for training for the Babylonian civil service. He makes no objection to serving a pagan emperor in this way. He makes no objection to immersing himself in the 'literature and language of the Chaldees' (Dan 1:4), literature that was predominantly idolatrous in orientation. He makes no objection to being given a new name that commemorates the pagan deity Bel. In sum, Daniel is not a superspiritual individual who refuses to interact with the surrounding culture. There is, however, one area in which he resolves not to compromise. He won't consume the rich food and wine stipulated as the appropriate diet for budding civil servants. To Daniel this would mean defiling himself.

Daniel's approach to the problem is respectful and highly creative. First, he asks permission of the official in charge of his well-being. Second, he takes the official's responsibilities and obligations into account. It is the official's job to keep the future imperial bureaucracy healthy. If he fails to do so, he may lose his job or his head. Daniel proposes a test: we'll eat vegetables and drink water for ten days, and then you'll be able to see if we are sufficiently healthy to continue doing so. It was a test that acknowledged the official's concerns – long enough to show results but not so long as to endanger the connection between the official's head and his shoulder-blades. A creative, negotiated solution where both sides won.

## WHOSE EMPLOYEES ARE WE ANYWAY?

So we seek to obey our boss, not because we are slaves to men but because we are slaves of Christ:

> For he who was a slave when he was called by the Lord is the Lord's freedman; similarly, he who was a free man when he was called is Christ's slave. You were bought at a price; do not become slaves of men.
>
> *I Corinthians 7:22–23*

Our primary allegiance is to Christ – we serve *him*. One of the ways we do this is by serving our boss. The incentive for our service is not our boss's power but reverence for Christ:

> Slaves, obey your earthly masters in everything;
> and do it, not only when their eye is on you and
> to win their favour, but with sincerity of heart
> and reverence for the Lord.
>
> *Colossians 3:22*

This is a radical call and Paul reinforces it in the following two verses:

> Whatever you do, work at it with all your heart,
> as working for the Lord, not for men, since you
> know that you will receive an inheritance from
> the Lord as a reward.

So, when you work the extra hours and no one notices, do you consider that you will receive an inheritance from the Lord as a reward? And when your boss asks you to do something, do you see Christ standing behind her saying, 'Do it for me'? Or do you resent her and perhaps sometimes even go so far as to blame all the frustration of a particular task – the rain, the mud, the equipment that hasn't arrived and the short tempers of the rest of the team – on the boss who gave you the task in the first place?

## FUTURE BLOCK?

The second reason many of us feel tension with our boss is that we believe our whole destiny lies in her hands. The boss decides whether I get a pay rise, whether I keep my job, whether I get promoted. But is this true?

Psalm 93:1 begins, 'The Lord reigns...' Indeed, the ultimate sovereignty of God is a consistent theme throughout the Bible. But does he reign over my career prospects?

The Bible makes it clear that God is in control of our bosses. He may not always choose to exercise that power, but he can:

> The king's heart is in the hand of the Lord;
> he directs it like a watercourse wherever he
> pleases.
>
> Proverbs 21:1

God may well use that sovereign power for your benefit. Just as he used the Babylonians to accomplish his purposes in the people of Israel (Jer 25:1–14), so he may use your boss to accomplish his purposes in you. He is sovereign and he loves you, and all things work together 'for the good of those who love him, who have been called according to his purpose' (Rom 8:28).

This has some startling implications. If God is sovereign and wants the best for you, then the boss you have is the boss God wants you to have. The boss you have is the perfect boss for you right now. God is a teacher, and he is using that person in your life to teach you.

The question is, what does he want to teach you? What are you meant to be learning?

## BOSS – TAILOR-MADE?

Your boss is not an unfortunate obstacle in your path to spiritual maturity, but far more likely to be an instrument in God's hand to bring about that spiritual maturity. God is in control of our bosses. And he is in control even when they have lost control, when circumstances arise in which they are unable to act on our behalf even though they might want to.

Again Daniel's life provides an example of an employee whose boss has completely lost control of a situation (Dan 6). Daniel is working for Darius, the third emperor he has served, and he has done such an outstanding job that Darius plans, as we saw earlier, to make him chief administrator of the entire empire. The plan provokes Daniel's colleagues to try to find a way to discredit him.

Finding no fault in his performance or morality, they are forced to devise a scheme to discredit him through his faith in the God of Israel. They persuade the king to sign a decree that anyone who prays to any god or man except to the king for the following thirty days should be thrown into the lions' den.

Daniel refuses to comply with the edict. His colleagues report the matter to the king, reminding him of the inviolability of the law – not even he can repeal a law once it is given. Reluctantly the king consigns Daniel to the lions, but with a sincere wish: 'May your God, whom you serve continually, rescue you'. That night the king fasts.

Darius has lost control of the situation. He finds himself, even as emperor, unable to protect his employee. God, however, is able and intervenes decisively.

The belief that our boss has our future in her hands stands in direct contradiction to the Bible. Our future is in fact determined by: God's plan for our lives, and our response to God as his plan unfolds.

Moses is a murderer with limited public-speaking skills. He is also an experienced shepherd with a tremendous love for his people. Most importantly, however, he responds to God's revelation of himself and to his commands. And he becomes leader of the people of Israel (Exod 1–4).

Daniel begins as just one of a group of young Israelite scholars. And becomes chief administrator.

David is just a young shepherd, indeed the youngest son in a large family. And he becomes king of Israel.

God is in charge:

> For neither from the east nor from the west, nor
> from the desert does promotion come; but God
> is the judge. He puts one down and promotes
> another.
>
> *Psalm 75:6–7, New Berkeley Version*

## THE WAY UP IS SOMETIMES DOWN

As far as promotion is concerned, I have had my ups and downs. On one occasion I was promised an early promotion. But, for reasons beyond my immediate boss's control, it kept on being delayed. I felt jerked around, lost perspective and started to become resentful. Instead of enjoying the fact that I was going to be given new responsibilities in due course, I became focused on my promotion happening as soon as possible. It began to occupy far too much of my thinking time, probably adversely affecting my performance. Why was I so anxious? So wound up? Was it lust for recognition? Quite probably.

On another occasion four people of roughly similar experience were promoted and I wasn't. I was pretty upset, but I soon realised I wasn't actually terribly interested in doing the next job up at that time and I was simply suffering from wounded pride. Shortly afterwards I was asked to co-direct the training programme – an experience of immense joy that I would have missed had I been promoted earlier.

On a third occasion, however, I was furious. I had recently had a stellar evaluation from my immediate boss. She had told me, and I jest not, that I could 'become a giant in the industry, if I wanted to'. A few weeks later six people got promoted and I didn't. If I was a giant, how come I was being treated like a dwarf?

Heaven knows no fury like an adman scorned. My anger seethed like a volcano on the brink of explosion, erupting late at night in long soliloquies addressed to my bedroom ceiling. Impassioned paragraphs of measured, invincible logic on the facts of the matter, my own galactic achievements, the machiavellian machinations that had lead to this miscarriage of justice, the vacuum of discernment that had precipitated this ignominious betrayal of talent and loyalty, the weakness of character that had led to this pathetic pandering to the squeaking wheedlers oiling their way up the ladder of power. I had, in my view, been stabbed in the back. I thought angry thoughts to God: 'I trusted you. I gave you my career. Now look what a mess you've made of it'.

But he was there. At the train station, the ticket-seller responded to my offer of a tract with a pat on the hand and some kind words. The very evening of the catastrophe, when I arrived home and forced myself resentfully to open my Bible, the first words I saw were from Psalm 37: 'Fret not'. Like a father to an over-wrought child.

Don't be anxious. It made me laugh and put things into some kind of perspective, temporarily at least. It had been easy to memorise the verse about God exalting one and putting down another. It turned out to be much harder to apply it. Through that experience, however, I became wiser. God taught me that I had been somewhat naive: I had failed to manage my career, failed to communicate to those above me where I wanted to go. I had seen the company as a benevolent parent who would always be fair, rather than as an inevitably flawed group of people, doing their best to juggle the interests of the company with the interests of their clients and the interests of individual employees. And besides, I had to ask myself the question: is someone who doesn't know how to manage senior people within the company the right person to interact with senior clients?

I saw the company as a benevolent parent partly because of the way that I tend to respond to authority. I am inclined, except when covered with cake, to avoid disagreement and to bottle up feelings of anger. At its worst this tendency can lead to a failure to contradict the boss, even when you know what she is proposing is downright wrong. Conversely, more independent types may overreact in the opposite direction and see the boss as the enemy, and secretly or openly rebel against any limitation of their independence. Neither is healthy.

## NO GUARANTEES

In my case, other opportunities for promotion came – but they might not have. God does honour those who honour him, but there is absolutely no guarantee of success, no guarantee that we won't be fired or passed over. We can never take his grace for granted. The call is always to follow him. Whether to a painful death on a cross like the apostle Peter, or like many Sudanese Christians in the last few years. Or to a long life like the disciple John or Billy Graham.

The conviction that God is the boss is, in fact, liberating. Faced by an intensely irritating manager or an impulsive, tyrannical foreman we can ask ourselves, how is my real boss treating me?

## LOOKING AFTER NUMBER TWO?

At one point I had a boss who was, I felt, lazy, unreasonable, untalented, a creative craftsman of the truth, a glory-seeker and a chauvinist. I was, you might say, 'uncomfortable with his management style'. At least that's how I saw it at the time.

Suddenly, two thoughts struck me.

First, I put my boss in perspective. OK, this man isn't treating me that well, or at least so I thought, but how is my real boss treating me? Apart from dying for me and sending me the Holy Spirit. And blessing me with a good church. And giving me a fine pastor and a marvellous discipler. And a lovely family. And great friends. And a nice place to live. In an exciting city. And, on the whole, great people to work with. Not to mention health and food and pots of money. My real boss was being lavish in his generosity. And the relationship with my boss at work, though significant, was a tiny puff of cloud in an ocean of azure sky.

The second thought that struck me was this – this lazy, unreasonable, machiavellian office politician, this creative craftsman of the truth, this glory-seeking chauvinist is someone God loves. How could that be? Jesus died for this person. Was I even praying for him? Was I giving him a chance?

I had been on the business a year and knew the clients well. I was liked and respected. Then he came. Did I really support him? Help him learn the business?

The result of my lack of support for my boss might well have been that when I had a problem I couldn't resolve, and I really needed someone higher up, I had so undermined my boss he didn't have the credibility with the clients to help me.

Which one of us was the jerk really?

I hadn't taken the time to teach him the business. I hadn't considered his insecurity in a new and demanding role. I wasn't prepared to let go of my status to help him establish himself. I was focused on looking good myself rather than on making him look good. On looking good myself rather than doing what was best for the business. I was too focused on looking after number one to remember that I was actually meant to be number two.

I didn't think about his strengths, didn't think about how to improve the way we worked together, didn't think about how to make our different work-styles as productive as possible for the business. Furthermore, I wasn't prepared to tell him the problems I had with him. He might not have been a great boss, but I wasn't doing too well being the perfect subordinate.

A servant heart would not have shown up in an autopsy.

So, although I thought I was the innocent party, I had made a significant contribution to the problem. Certainly we got on quite well, but underneath the surface jollity lurked a bubbling sea of resentments that I was hardly aware of and was almost certainly unwilling to admit to myself. The bottom line was that I had certainly not treated him with anything like authentic love.

## BLUEPRINT FOR THE RADICAL EMPLOYEE

The biblical model for both the employer and the employee is a servant model – one who deploys his gifts and resources for the benefit of another person. Christ is the supreme example of this. It is he we must seek to imitate:

> Be imitators of God, therefore, as dearly loved
> children and live a life of love, just as Christ loved
> us and gave himself up for us as a fragrant offer-
> ing and sacrifice to God.
>
> *Ephesians 5:1–2*

Christ consistently recognised God's authority – and he acts in line with his Father's will:

> 'I tell you the truth, the Son can do nothing by
> himself; he can do only what he sees his Father
> doing, because whatever the Father does the Son
> also does.'
>
> *John 5:19*

Jesus' teaching is not his own – 'It comes from him who sent me' (John 7:16). He does not seek glory for himself (John 8:50) but gives God the credit. He gains his reward and significance from God.

## BRICKS WITHOUT STRAW?

Christ calls us to go one step further in our relationship with our employers:

> 'So you also, when you have done everything you were told to do, should say, "We are unworthy servants; we have only done our duty."'
>
> *Luke 17:10*

This is not a mandate for longer hours, or for the workaholism that plagues some people, or for acceptance of the crushing pressure that some companies bring to bear on their employees, but rather a summons to a willing, thoughtful attitude. As Paul writes in another context, 'The Lord loves a cheerful giver'. The true servant isn't simply seeking to fulfil his obligations but to serve, to be looking out for ways of helping his employer, to make his employer's job easier.

One of the keys to working well with our boss is to know his expectations and to understand his preferred way of working. And to adapt accordingly. Some bosses like a lot of information, some don't like much. Some like written reports and recommendations, some prefer discussion. Some are very much hands-on, some prefer to delegate. Know your boss. This has nothing to do with political manoeuvring but everything to do with getting the job done as efficiently as possible. As Gabarro and Kotter pointed out in the *Harvard Business Review* 1979, knowing how to manage upwards is a vital part of getting the job done well. You and your boss are in a relationship. You are both fallible. You both need each other. Work at getting it right.

Is your relationship with your boss creative and dynamic? Do you love your boss as yourself? Do you pray for her? Do you deal creatively and courageously with the things she does that bother you? Do you support her? Do you recognise your responsibility to submit to her authority even though you may need to challenge some of her decisions? Do you know her expectations? Do you seek to work out ways to make your working relationship as productive as possible? Do you believe that it is God who is in charge of your career, and that he will use your workplace and your boss to accomplish his purposes in your life?

Quite often I didn't.

• • •

## • EPILOGUE •
### Fighting back?

It was the morning after the night before.

I'd got most of the cream off my suit – the dry cleaners would do the rest. There'd been several phone calls from people who worked with me and there hadn't been much sleep. Now it was time to go to work.

I knew what I was supposed to do.

I knew what I had to do.

I had to get in early and go and see my boss – at least the one I had propelled across a restaurant in front of his staff – and I had to apologise. I had no idea how he would react. Understandably, he had been angry the night before when we talked outside the restaurant. Even more understandably, since he in fact hadn't contributed any of his birthday cake to my suit.

I knocked on his door. He said, 'Come in', and turned

round from his desk to face me. I could see the tension in his face. I sat down opposite him and apologised, and said that there was no excuse for the way I had reacted. I could see the tension disappear from his face. He accepted my apology without reproving me at all, and said that that was the end of the matter.

It was. He never mentioned it again.

He treated me just as fairly and firmly and generously as he had before.

Indeed, after he left the agency to work elsewhere, he twice called me up to offer me a job in his new company.

It remains one of the most startling incidents of forgiveness I have ever experienced.

● ● ●

# • 11 •

## REBEL, REBEL

### or
### No hard feelings?

*'How can you say to your brother,*
*"Let me take the speck out of your eye,"*
*when all the time there is a plank*
*in your own eye?'*

Matthew 7:4

This chapter is, if you like, a time for you to pause and reflect on some of your attitudes to authority in general and to your boss in particular. In seminars I have taught, I have found that this exercise is helpful and sometimes surprising for people. You may discover attitudes you never knew were there. And sometimes even attitudes you definitely thought were *not* there.

For the most part this chapter contains verses from scripture unadorned by commentary. Read them slowly perhaps and see if the Holy Spirit brings something to mind as you consider for yourself how these verses might apply to you.

• • •

- Our boss's authority is from God and we are to submit to it.

  Everyone must submit himself to the governing authorities, for there is no authority except that which God has established. The authorities that exist have been established by God.

  *Romans 13:1*

- We submit to our boss's authority to adorn the Good News.

  Teach slaves to be subject to their masters in everything, to try to please them, not to talk back to them, and not to steal from them, but to show that they can be fully trusted, so that in every way they will make the teaching about God our Saviour attractive.

  *Titus 2:9–10*

- God is our real boss.

  Whatever you do, work at it with all your heart, as working for the Lord, not for men, since you know that you will receive an inheritance from the Lord as a reward. It is the Lord Christ you are serving.

  *Colossians 3:23–24*

- God is in control of our careers, promotions, success and failure.

  For neither from the east, nor from the west, nor from the desert does promotion come; but God is the judge. He puts down one and promotes another.

  *Psalm 75:6, 7; New Berkeley Version*

- God loves your boss.

For God so loved the world that he gave his one
and only Son, that whoever believes in him shall
not perish but have eternal life.

*John 3:16*

- We shouldn't criticise our boss publicly or encourage complaints.

An example: Absalom's public criticism of
David, his father (2 Sam 15:1–6). The situation:
Absalom, harboring anger against David, spends
four years standing by the road on the way up to
the city, ingratiating himself with passers-by and
promising them 'favourable' justice – if only he
were appointed judge in the land. Of course, if I
were in charge of this business, all would be well...

- We owe our boss outward and heart-felt loyalty,
regardless of whether it's beneficial to us in the
short-term.

An example: Ittai the Gittite (2 Sam 15:14–23).
The situation: after years of trying to undermine
David's authority, Absalom has finally rebelled
openly. David is forced to flee from Jerusalem. Ittai
the Gittite and his 600 men are with him. Ittai is
not an Israelite, he has no binding obligation to
stand with David against Absalom, and he only
arrived in Jerusalem the day before the rebellion
broke out. Furthermore, David has expressly
released him from any duty to go with him. But
Ittai has made a commitment to David. It's a commitment that may well result in his death but it's
one that he sticks by:

'As surely as the Lord lives, and as my lord the
king lives, wherever my lord the king may be,
whether it means life or death, there will your
servant be.'

This is loyalty. And, though the circumstances are almost too extreme to find contemporary comparisons, what level of loyalty do you feel towards your boss?

- We need to make sure we have flushed out any unresolved anger, resentments or negative feelings. They lead to cake on the suit or perhaps a spear in the wall.

  To some significant extent I may well have been harbouring unconfessed resentments towards those in authority over me, which contributed to the intensity of my response to having cream cake daubed over my suit.

  Get rid of all bitterness, rage and anger, brawling and slander, along with every form of malice.

  *Ephesians 4:31*

• • •

## QUESTIONS TO ASK, VERSES TO CONSIDER

- Am I selfishly ambitious?

  For where you have envy and selfish ambition, there you find disorder and every evil practice.

  *James 3:16*

- Am I really considering my boss's needs?

  Do nothing out of selfish ambition or vain conceit, but in humility consider others better than yourselves. Each of you should look not only to your own interests, but also to the interests of others.

  *Philippians 2:3–4*

- Am I trying to take the credit?

For it is not the one who commends himself who is approved, but the one whom the Lord commends.

*2 Corinthians 10:18 (see also Luke 14:7–11)*

• Am I proud?

To fear the Lord is to hate evil;
    I hate pride and arrogance,
    evil behaviour and perverse speech.

*Proverbs 8:13*

• Am I really submitting to my boss's authority? Or simply doing what I'm told?

Teach slaves to be subject to their masters in everything, to try to please them, not to talk back to them...

*Titus 2:9*

• Do I genuinely forgive my boss when he does something wrong?

Be kind and compassionate to one another, forgiving each other, just as in Christ God forgave you.

*Ephesians 4:32 (see also Matthew 18:21–22)*

• Do I love my boss and actively seek opportunities to express that love?

Dear children, let us not love with words or tongue but with actions and in truth.

*1 John 3:18*

• Do I fail to see opportunities in apparently adverse circumstances?

Consider it pure joy, my brothers, whenever you face trials of many kinds, because you know that the testing of your faith develops perseverance.

*James 1:2–3*

Now I want you to know, brothers, that what has happened to me has really served to advance the gospel. As a result, it has become clear throughout the whole palace guard and to everyone else that I am in chains for Christ. Because of my chains, most of the brothers in the Lord have been encouraged to speak the word of God more courageously and fearlessly.

*Philippians 1:12–14*

* Do I communicate my problems with my boss to him? And do I do this lovingly?

Instead, speaking the truth in love, we will in all things grow up into him who is the Head, that is, Christ.

*Ephesians 4:15*

* The principle of Matthew 18:15 probably also applies, even though the original context relates to problems between Christians:

If your brother sins against you, go and show him his fault, just between the two of you. If he listens to you, you have won your brother over.

• • •

As you have reflected on your relationship with your boss, what discoveries have you made?

If we confess our sins, he is faithful and just and will forgive us our sins and purify us from all unrighteousness.

*1 John 1:9*

# • 12 •

# LIFE ON THE CRASH BARRIER

## or
## Peace in the maelstrom?

*As far as work is concerned I feel like the bus in Speed. I'm doing more than 50mph in a built-up area. If I stop, I and a whole lot of other people are going to get blown up. If I keep going, sooner or later I'm going to hit something, and I and a whole lot of other people are going to get blown up.*

It used to be life in the fast lane, but now for many working people it feels like life on the crash barrier.

It's not just the longer hours and the sense that you have to do them or get fired. It's not just the feeling that my business, company, organisation isn't as much fun as it used to be. It's not just the suspicion that every time a group of people are trained to handle a new technology, two or three of them will not, in the click of a mouse, be around to use it.

It's not just stress, or at least it's not just something that can be solved by doing all the helpful things that stress-counsellors advise us to do – eat better, take exercise, take time to relax, plan, and so on.

There's anxiety in the air. It may be true, as *Management Today* recently reported, that we are all actually more secure in our jobs than we thought but we'll never take security for granted again. Just as, after the great negative-equity crash in the housing market, no one will ever again say, 'You can't lose on property'. Redundancy insurance is here to stay. Jobs for life in the same company are increasingly becoming a curiosity and, for some people, staying a long time in one company can be seen as a weakness. Not good enough to move, eh? Not ambitious enough, eh?

The anxiety about job security is part of a much wider atmosphere of uncertainty and radical change. If you're over forty, you probably began your working life believing there would always be a good education for your children, there would always be a reliable health service, there would always be a decent state pension... Well, we no longer have those assurances, do we?

And all that uncertainty, all that turn-over of people, not only creates its own tension for us, it radically affects how we regard the people around us. They aren't potential colleagues for life, they're here today and probably gone tomorrow. Why bother developing relationships? Why tell the truth? Why be loyal? Why build this business for the long term? I'm not even going to be here to see the medium term.

Many companies have radically changed their perspectives on recruitment. Now they work on the basis that 75% of the people they recruit will be gone in four or five years and that those people know it. So, in an attempt to get the best people, they recruit on the basis of how easy it will be for their employees to get jobs when they leave. Furthermore, some companies, the less enlightened ones to be sure, have become used to being hard-nosed, accustomed to seeing redundancy as a solution, rather than really asking themselves whether there aren't opportunities to use those people to develop business in new areas. It's not always possible but it's worth looking into.

Recently Gerald went into an avionics company as a consultant. They told him the solution they wanted: 'Close this department down. Make this lot redundant'. He wasn't going to take £1,000 a day to rubber-stamp a foregone conclusion, so he refused to go in on that basis. They hired him anyway, and he came back with a recommendation for redeployment that would save jobs and enable the company to grow in a particular sector.

Work has changed. There is a massive increase in the number of people working on their own: freelancers, consultants of various kinds with a portfolio of skills and clients, people who are called in to fill a short-term gap and then let go, people working from home.

This new, looser self-employed structure is here to stay but it isn't necessarily comfortable.

Suddenly, we are all being forced to realise that the harvest may not come in, that there could be a sudden frost, that the locusts may stream over the mountains on the chill wind of a corporate restructuring, an overseas competitor, an innovation in technology. Suddenly we have come to realise that our wages, our salaries are not so certain, that for all our trust in BT or BP, our companies are only the channel for God's provision, not the source. Our provision always comes from him. We are dependent. And if we're honest, we don't much like it. At least not to begin with.

David tests sophisticated electrical equipment. He does it freelance from what can only be described as a bunker in his home. With 20,000 volts or so zooming round the room, you knock before entering. He has three kids and a mortgage and never knows where the money is coming from in two weeks' time. He has to keep up with his field, he has to do a good job and, from his perspective, he has to trust God to bring him clients.

## LIVING BY THE RAILWAY

So we live with uncertainty.

If we're of a calm disposition then we're like people who live by railway tracks, no longer disturbed by freight trains clanking away all through the night.

If, on the other hand, we're of an anxious disposition then we're like overnight guests in the houses of people who live by railway tracks with freight trains clanking away all through the night. We come down the next morning, eyes bleary and black-rimmed from lack of sleep, stumbling irritably towards the coffee.

'Sleep well?' our hostess asks brightly.

'Like a log,' we reply, British courtesy once again winning over the impulse to tell the truth.

What we are facing in the West is beginning to feel like a return to the first part of the century, when the dockers would go down to the wharf at 6 o'clock in the morning to find out whether today there would be work and tonight there would be butter on the bread. We are facing uncertainty.

Uncertainty can steal the joy of work. It's not fun putting everything into a job when you're not sure it's going to be there in a year's time.

Uncertainty can steal the joy of success. Last year one of the Big Four banks posted record profits and awarded its employees an 8% bonus. But morale remained low. People were making money but had little sense of security. If you take away hope for the future, the present loses its savour. As it says in Proverbs 12:25, 'An anxious heart weighs a man down'.

Uncertainty turns colleagues into rivals.

Uncertainty turns bosses into potential executioners.

And it affects business. A survey in an oil company in Brussels in 1993 concluded that 60% of the ailments suffered by people in the company – ailments that naturally affected performance to some degree or another – were caused by anxiety.

Some companies attempt to deal with the symptoms. One London merchant bank knows their people are stressed by the demands of extremely long hours. They won't change that but there's a masseuse in the building. Other companies are looking at ways they can reduce the divorce rate among their employees.

Some companies don't care about the long hours. As one manager put it, 'I don't mind that my people are working such long hours because I've been told I have to reduce head count. Long hours mean that some of them can't take it anymore and they resign. Which is a lot cheaper than making them redundant.'

'Are you anxious?' For years, this question didn't seem to apply:

> '...do not worry about your life, what you will eat or drink; or about your body, what you will wear ... do not worry about tomorrow, for tomorrow will worry about itself.'
>
> *Matthew 6:25, 34*

I wasn't anxious about tomorrow, at least not about material things, about what I would eat or wear. I was young, single and working in advertising. Wearing Italian suits and eating in Manhattan restaurants.

Now, things are different. I'm older, marvellously married, splendidly endowed with three children, and I work for a Christian organisation which, though the best theological college in the world, isn't exactly doling out Ferraris for annual bonuses. A while back I calculated that if I were in management, and I am, and if the best theological college in the world had to make people redundant, I'd be the second to go. Later, after longer reflection and deeper, entirely objective analysis

I concluded that I would be crazy to let myself go. Fortunately, so far we haven't had to make anyone redundant. But occasionally I wonder whether I will make it to retirement. I need to, because if my children go to college I'll be 63 or 64 when the last one gets out.

Insecurity can change our agenda. Worry about money can dominate us rather than a daily concern to seek first his kingdom and his righteousness. Keeping our job can dominate our thinking rather than the desire to do the job well. Being seen to do well becomes more important than doing well. Other people become less important.

Anxiety makes us more focused on ourselves, less focused on serving our boss, more on winning our boss.

As we worry about tomorrow, today slips away. But why should our work lose its joy? Why should we become less trusting of our colleagues and less helpful, or more concerned to take the credit and quicker to assign blame elsewhere?

It is a time of radical social change. God's people have been through it before. From Egypt to the Promised Land. From Judah to Babylon. The temple destroyed, the land overrun, the king deposed and many of the people deported. All the old certainties a fading memory.

Will God now abandon us?

What does the carpenter know about sudden lake storms or corporate downsizing?

The reality is that we thought we were in charge of this area of our lives. We thought, like Jesus' fishermen disciples, that we were the experts, that we could get to the other side. But this area is out of our control, this area is no longer safe, this is an area we need to trust him for.

## PEACE FIRST

How can we have peace in an uncertain world?

In the West, our society works to achieve peace. We work to gain financial security, we work to gain the money to help us flourish as humans, we work to gain status, we work to develop relationships that affirm us and build us up. Our satisfaction comes from the work of our hands.

Now joy in our work is, as Ecclesiastes says, a gift from God. But the Christian doesn't work to gain peace. On the contrary, we gain our peace from our relationship with God. Our *shalom*, our wholeness, is in Christ. It grows out of our relationship with him, from being in the vine, from the certainty of his love, on the basis of his promises to us. It is from the *shalom* we already have in Christ that we go out into the world.

We don't run towards his rest. We run *in* his rest.

We don't go out to work to find our worth, we start work already in the knowledge of our worth in Christ.

We don't go to work to gain status, we go to work with the status of the sons and daughters of the king of the universe.

Rest in God, then move out to work with the strength and perspective he has provided...

Anxious? Well, according to John 'perfect love drives out fear' (1 John 4:18) The more we realise we are loved, the less we will fear. The more we realise we are loved by our tender heavenly Father, the less we will fear earthly authorities. What do I have to lose that my heavenly Father cannot replace and better?

Here is Paul's perspective:

> Do not be anxious about anything, but by prayer and petition, with thanksgiving, present your requests to God.

> *Philippians 4:6*

Paul is probably not talking about the kinds of chronic anxiety that have their roots in clinical depression but rather that general, though often deep, sense of uncertainty many of us feel. That said, he is giving us a command that has at least four components:

1   It is a command that recognises reality, that is, it recognises that we feel anxious.

2   It is a command that stipulates a priority. The solution to anxiety is not first and foremost action but prayer. Paul doesn't tell us to 'get on our bikes or our PCs and go solve the problem'. He tells us to get on our knees and give the problem to God. So we talk to God and we ask for what his Spirit prompts us to ask.

3   It is a command that demands trust. We can talk to God without trusting him. But we cannot thank him without trusting that he loves us, that he will do what is best. We cannot thank him without acknowledging his sovereignty. We give thanks in anticipation of the right answer from him.

4   It is a command that contains a promise. If we do this, then God will give us peace. It is not the peace the world gives. That peace is fragile and built on sand. It cannot stop us becoming anxious when the next problem arises. The peace God gives passes understanding precisely because anxiety might actually be the natural response.

Isn't it natural to be anxious when you may not have a job next year? Isn't it natural to be anxious when you may find yourself persecuted? Isn't it natural to be anxious if you are a coal dealer in an area that is about to be designated a smokeless zone?

It *is* natural. And that is why peace, that deep

spiritual serenity we see in some people, is so
startling.

It *isn't* natural. And because it isn't natural it is
an extraordinary witness.

If morale is low in your workplace but your joy
remains, if people have become niggly about management and critical of one another and you remain objective about management and generous to colleagues...
won't people recognise Christ in you?

When David was made redundant, it made him re-
evaluate his whole life. And it brought him to God.
Today he's a management consultant working for a
large company. Secure but not so very secure. Does he
feel anxious? His response: 'Having seen what God did
the first time round I don't worry about it'.

Of course, this deep trust doesn't mean that we
shouldn't take steps to plan for certain eventualities,
that we don't consider whether we should begin to
explore other job options or get further training. But it
does mean that we don't do it with fear burning an
ulcer in our belly.

Our non-Christian friends know only one thing
about their future for sure – they're going to die.

We're going to die too. But we know far more about
the end of our story – we know that we have been
called, and that we are loved by God the Father and
kept by Jesus Christ (Jude 1).

We know that we will die, but we know that we will
go to be with the Father.

We know that we will die but we know that we will
spend an eternity enjoying God.

There's one other thing we know: whatever happens
in the next episode of our story, we know who's in the
boat with us.

# LIES "R" US

### or
### Too true to be good

*A pocketful of mumbles, such are promises.*
*All lies and jests –*
*still a man hears what he wants to hear*
*and disregards the rest...*

Paul Simon, 'The Boxer'

Truth – who tells it? Our culture is pervaded with deceit, and we are programmed to distrust.

Deceit is everywhere.

'It's in the post. Didn't you get it?' No, it wasn't and we haven't. Beware – there are people out there who send the envelopes back, pointing out the date on the postmark.

Builders who do things for cash so the job remains undeclared. Taxi drivers who offer blank receipts so that I can charge a bit more on my expense account. The retailer who tells me that this little plastic widget for my Qualcast mower costs £3: we phone Qualcast and they say 16p. The man who comes to our door to sell us an aerial photo of our rather modest garden – £20. We demur; he says, 'I tell you what, I'll give it to you for £15 and tell my boss the frame was broken.'

Deceit taints our day-to-day dealings. In the research I have conducted, the pressure to be dishonest seems to be the number one moral issue facing Christians at work.

A while back, the University of Westminster surveyed company directors and came to the conclusion that the vast majority would break the law if they thought they could get away with it. In sum, honesty is not the issue. Companies are not assessing right and wrong: they are calculating risk.

It isn't just business. The story goes of a university head of department who rearranged the lecture timetable so that when the inspectors arrived the duff lecturers wouldn't be there to underperform.

It isn't just business and education. Marriage vows are spoken with fingers crossed and the prenuptial agreements quietly packed in the honeymoon luggage. And how is it that a godparent who isn't a Christian can make the promises contained in the Anglican christening service? But they do.

It's not just business, education and church vows. We distrust our politicians when they deliver strong lectures on upholding moral and family life but have affairs and apparently accept 'cash for questions'; when they wring their hands over wars happening around the world but don't want to risk losing the lucrative profits made by the arms trade; when they are quick to send troops against Saddam Hussein's powerful Iraqi forces to protect oil, but in Bosnia won't move against the relatively small Serbian army to protect Muslims.

We don't trust the police like we used to: the Birmingham Six, the Guildford Four, the Maguire Seven – case after case of apparently fabricated police evidence.

If we are in work and trying to stay true to Christ, it

is still hard not to be drawn into the web of other people's lies.

I am at an evening 'client and agency' party. One of the senior agency people is there with his wife. It is going to be complicated to meet her. I know something she doesn't. Her husband is having an affair with one of my colleagues. Everyone from the agency is aware of it.

We are introduced, we talk, and all the time I'm thinking the kind of thoughts you think. A mixture of pity, of ghastly fascination, of looking for a reason why it may be her fault – or his. All the while, having this dirty, clammy feeling that I too am deceiving her. That one day she will find out. One day she will know that we were all silent partners in his betrayal.

Deceit taints our day-to-day dealings.

## TRUTH IN THE CHURCH?

It isn't as if we find it easy to tell the truth in church.

The story goes of a visiting preacher in a local church. He preached the sermon and thought he had done quite well. At the door people shook his hand and made complimentary comments. Then one small, slightly odd-looking man said, 'You went on too long.'

Others followed with their compliments. Then the small man came back again – he was obviously not all there – and said, 'I didn't agree with you, you know.'

He disappeared again. More handshakes followed. He returned and said, 'Actually, I thought it was a load of old rubbish.'

He disappeared and returned once more saying, 'You really *did* go on far too long.'

Over lunch, the incumbent pastor asked the visitor how he thought it had gone.

'Fine. Everyone was very complimentary, except for

one man who came up to me four times to register various complaints. A rather odd-looking man.'

'Small man, older, not quite all there?' asked the pastor.

'That's right,' said the visitor.

'Oh, don't worry about him. He just goes around listening to what everyone else is saying, then comes and repeats it.'

Truth. We don't even tell it in the church, never mind in the world. We have acquired a habit of false courtesy and lost the ability to critique anyone, helpfully or unhelpfully.

Truth. We don't even tell it in the church. Partly because we have a false view of encouragement. We think it is encouraging to tell someone they have been helpful when they haven't. It isn't. It may be encouraging to focus on a person's good points to build up his or her confidence. But to mislead someone, week in, week out? That is not encouragement.

No wonder sermons have such a poor reputation in this country. Millions find them unhelpful, but the preachers don't know it. Millions find them boring, but I have yet to meet a preacher who thinks that he or she is boring.

Truth. We don't even tell it in the church.

Maybe it's because we have read Ephesians 4:15, about 'speaking the truth in love'. We have taken love to mean something it isn't. Love builds up. Love won't consign someone else to mediocrity.

We don't tell the truth in the church because we don't want to offend anyone. Maybe we have forgotten these verses in Proverbs:

> He who rebukes a man will in the end gain
> more favour
> than he who has a flattering tongue.
>
> *Proverbs 28:23*

> Wounds from a friend can be trusted,
> but an enemy multiplies kisses.
>
> *Proverbs 27:6*

One way or another, we are afraid of telling the truth. Of creating dynamics that allow the truth to emerge. No wonder it is hard to tell the truth at work if we can't find ways of doing it in our own communities.

## SOME BIBLICAL FOUNDATIONS

Truth in the Bible is an active, dynamic idea. It is something to be done, not something to nod at in mere assent. Truth relates closely to truthfulness, faithfulness, consistency. God is true not just in the sense that he exists, but in the sense that he is not false, unreliable or unfaithful. God's word is reliable not just in the sense that it is objectively true and you can trust his motives, but also in the sense that his word will come true. If he says he will be there, it means he will be there.

This understanding of truth as embracing future reliability as well as present intent has shattered any illusion I had of being a biblically truthful person.

An example. When I say, 'I'll get it done by Monday', I mean it at the moment I say it. But I probably haven't fully weighed the implications of what I have promised.

Can I actually deliver? Yes, if I don't get interrupted. Yes, if nothing unforeseen happens.

But I will be interrupted, won't I? Something unforeseen almost always happens. I don't take my word seriously enough. My 'Yes' is not 'Yes' and my 'No' is not 'No' (Matt 5:37). My 'Yes' is 'I hope so'. Or my 'Yes' is 'I like you and I don't want to disappoint you. Right now it's much easier for me to say "Yes" and bask in your smile of appreciation, than to say "No" and risk your irritation.' If my 'Yes' were really 'Yes', I would be thinking, 'Yes, they *will* have it on Monday. When I'm interrupted, or when something unforeseen happens, I'll work over the weekend to ensure that my "Yes" *is* "Yes".'

Had I considered seriously the implications of saying, 'You'll have it on Monday'? No, I hadn't. And I hadn't because I don't take seriously the idea of keeping my word.

Will I keep my word, even though it hurts? Psalm 15 says:

> Lord, who may dwell in your sanctuary?
>    Who may live on your holy hill?
>
> He whose walk is blameless
>    and who does what is righteous,
> who speaks the truth from his heart
>    and has no slander on his tongue,
> who does his neighbour no wrong
>    and casts no slur on his fellow-man,
> who despises a vile man
>    but who honours those who fear the Lord...

And here's the zinger:

> ...who keeps his oath
>    even when it hurts...
>
> He who does these things
>    will never be shaken.

God is truth.

Jesus is the way, the truth and the life. He speaks the truth. He sustains the truth. He lives the truth. He is the truth.

The Holy Spirit is called the Spirit of truth, given to guide us into all truth.

Verse after verse in the Bible puts an emphasis on

truth. 'Therefore love truth and peace' (Zech 8:19). 'What does God desire?' asks David: 'truth in the inner parts' (Psalm 51:6). What sort of worship does he seek? Worship 'in spirit and in truth' (John 4:24).

The antithesis of truth is not error but lies, deception. Not just something that is incorrect, but something that is untrustworthy, which gives a false picture of a person or situation, as Satan does. If truth is God's territory, then lies are the devil's. Jesus called him the father of lies (John 8:44). He lies and he generates lies.

After Adam rebels against God by eating the forbidden fruit, he begins to tell lies: 'It was the woman you gave me,' he claims, blaming God for giving him Eve rather than accepting his own responsibility.

The apostle Paul charts the dark, decadent, downward dive into depravity of a debauched pagan society, saying that it all begins with the suppression of truth (Rom 1:18–32). A lie corrupts the person telling it as well as deceiving those who hear it.

## WHY LIE?

We lie because we are afraid. Afraid of losing our jobs in a hostile environment where finding another job may be difficult.

Lying to escape negative consequences is a skill we learn early. Most of us can lie before we can talk.

Splattered with banana custard, a toddler sits on a floor that is also splattered with the contents of an upturned bowl. He looks cute. 'Did you do that?' you ask in a silky soft voice that belies the seismic upheaval stirring within. He looks up at you from beneath his long blond lashes, a dash of custard dripping off his fringe. He wags his head from side to side.

We lie to escape blame, to escape embarrassment.

We lie because we want to get on. To be loved,

admired, adored, accepted. To look good to others.

Some lie because they just don't care about truth. Some lie because it works. Some lie because it's a thrill.

Truthfulness builds trust: lies destroy it. Lies steal joy, destroy relationships, wreck society.

Lies create work for lawyers and legislators. In the City, a gentleman's word used to be his bond. These days the bond is junk, and no one can be trusted. So in the City there are now far more regulations. If I'm doing a deal, I have to assume that you may take advantage of me. You have to assume the same. I don't trust you, so I appoint lawyers to draft the contracts in order to prevent either of us doing what we ought to have had no intention of doing in the first place. Contracts that are getting longer and more expensive by the year.

## TAYLORING THE TRUTH?

Janette Taylor works as a secretary in a military establishment, the kind of place where an order is an order and you expect it to be obeyed. She is a civilian, but she works in a command culture.

The phone rings. It's for her boss. She tells him that so-and-so is on the line. He says, as do thousands of people all over Britain every day, 'Tell him I'm out.'

Janette says, 'I can't do that. You're not.'

There is a pause.

She continues, 'If I lie *for* you, you won't know when I'm lying *to* you.'

A few weeks later, another senior officer asks her to do something slightly shady. Janette says, 'You know I can't do that.'

He grins back: 'Yes, I know. I was just testing.'

Janette's case is perhaps quite simple, but it reflects a deep determination not to be compromised. Life is not always so straightforward. Can we develop a framework for truth-telling?

## WHEN IS A LIE NOT A LIE?

'How are you doing?' people used to ask me in the corridors of my New York workplace.

In the early days, I would start to answer: 'Fine, thank you. I'm settling in, and the work is interesting, and the people...'

But by this time my audience would be half way to Las Vegas. They hadn't been asking me a question: they were simply grunting cordially in my direction. A nod would have been response enough – even if my apartment had been burgled, my leg broken and I'd just discovered Tottenham had lost one nil to Arsenal.

Some questions aren't asking for the information they seem to be asking for. This is why we feel the need to supplement questions like 'How are you?' with questions like 'No, how are you *really*?' Every culture has these conversational conventions, and they are a convenient way of protecting our privacy. They are greetings, not questions, so you are not necessarily lying when you don't answer 'How are you?' with a detailed account of your emotional, physical and spiritual condition.

## NEGOTIATING CONVENTIONS

Conventions apply to most negotiating situations. These conventions can be abused, but we are usually aware of what they are supposed to be.

The Bible's first real-estate negotiation involves Abraham (Gen 23:1–16). He is trying to buy a cave in which to bury Sarah, his wife. He is negotiating with Ephron the Hittite, who appears to be offering him a free field...

'No, my lord,' he said, 'Listen to me; I give you the
field, and I give you the cave that is in it. I give it
to you in the presence of my people. Bury your
dead.'

But Ephron isn't offering Abraham a free field. In about
seven point two seconds he is going to ask 400 shekels
for it.

Ephron isn't lying to Abraham when he offers him a
free field. They both know he isn't offering a free field.
The offer is a cultural convention, rather like when a
middle-class Englishman is offered a second helping of
a creamy, meringuey, Mount-Everest-like pavlova. He
says, 'No, thank you. I couldn't possibly.' But he does-
n't mean 'No'. The consumption of another piece of
pavlova is not only well within his capacity, he is hop-
ing with all his heart that he will shortly have the
opportunity to demonstrate what an arrant liar he is. If
you don't ask him again, you are likely to be treated to
a howl of anguish not heard since the hound of the
Baskervilles bayed across the mist-laden moor of yes-
teryear. It is to avoid this blood-curdling wail that middle-class English hosts and hostesses have been brought
up to press their guest again and, if necessary, again,
until they do what they were always expected to do.

Similar conventions apply to many contemporary
negotiating situations. The problem arises when people
are no longer sure what the conventions are.

'That's my final bid' used to mean – *that's my final
bid*.

'Is it?' you ask your boss.

'Yes,' she says, 'it is my final bid, *for right now*.'

In other words, if it is refused, she may have another
final bid. But does the negotiator on the other side
know this?

In some situations, the fact that conventions can

change undermines important professional relationships. For example, within the health-care sector,
patients have gained the impression – by what they pick
up from medical programmes on TV – that there are
doctors who apply a 'need to know' policy when communicating information. If the patient doesn't need to
know, the doctor won't tell, even if asked. So the
patients begin to wonder if they really are being told
the truth about their condition, and this uncertainty
may be the cause of considerable anxiety.

The point isn't what actually is NHS practice, but
rather that the confusion of changing conventions can
create unnecessary distress. In reality, current medical
practice applies the principle that, if a patient asks for
information, he or she is usually ready to receive it –
good news or bad. And the wishes of the sick person
are put before those of his or her relatives.

Do other people understand the convention you are
operating within? Or are you deliberately using the
ambiguity of the convention to gain the advantage?

## CUTHBERT'S CODE

Some kinds of convention are inevitable. However not
all conventions are necessary.

Phil Cuthbert used to work in purchasing. He joined
a large manufacturing company, and decided to get rid
of what he calls 'the 21-day lie'. It goes something like
this.

You ring up and order some parts for a computer.
You say you need them on 1 June. You ask the supplier,
'Can you deliver?' The supplier thinks, 'He doesn't
mean 1 June – he means 22 June, but he's building in
time for me to be late. I can deliver by 18 June, so I'll
say 'Yes, I can deliver.'

Phil decided this was an unnecessary convention,

and he informed his suppliers one by one that when he asked for 1 June, he meant 1 June. He wasn't building in any time-gap. When he said that was the deadline, he meant that was the deadline. There would be no lifeline after that.

Phil took his words seriously, and he expected his suppliers to do the same. Some didn't, and they received calls the day before the deadline asking whether the materials would be ready.

'Yes,' they would say.

'Good,' said Phil on one occasion, 'I'll come and pick them up myself tomorrow morning.' His own hunch is that the factory worked all night to get his order ready, because ready it wasn't.

Naturally Phil was in a position of power because he could call the shots. But even when we are trying hard to live by our own code, we can blow it. For Phil, the crunch came one Monday. He realised he had completely forgotten about a piece of work he had promised his boss for that very day. There was no way he could get it done in time.

Most of us would have probably have scrambled through as quickly as possible, delivered the work late, but not said anything to our boss. Phil went to his boss, told him what had happened, apologised, gave him a date by which the work would be complete – and watched his boss's jaw drop in amazement.

## APPROVED LIES

In the Bible, some people tell lies and God doesn't seem to disapprove.

Rahab the prostitute lied to her fellow-citizens about the whereabouts of the two Israelite spies hiding in her roof (Joshua 2). She is hailed as a heroine of faith by the writer to the Hebrews (Heb 11:31).

The Hebrew midwives lied to Pharaoh when he asked them why they had disobeyed his order to kill new-born male babies (Exod 1:15–22). The principle of preserving life overrode the principle of telling the truth. Sometimes we are asked a question by someone who has, in a sense, no right to the truth – they will only use it to further their evil purposes. In this instance, a more important moral imperative takes over. Why should the Hebrew midwives have felt any obligation to tell the truth to a murderous dictator who was intent on the destruction of their own people?

Conversely, if I am in good relationship with an employer, I may feel it right to disclose information to him before my contract requires it, because to do so will help him make a wise decision. When I decided to resign from the New York office of Ogilvy and Mather, I gave five months' notice instead of the requisite three. It gave them more time to find someone else, and it prevented them appointing me to a new account that I would have had to leave just as I had learned the ropes.

Obvious, you may say. Indeed, but only when you are working for an employer you can trust. Because if they are untrustworthy, they may force you to leave after three months and save a bit of money. Similarly, if you are a married woman on a business trip with your boss and he asks, 'Have you any plans for children?', your response may be shaped by whether you feel this is a friendly question from a trusted colleague, or a strategic question from an employer intent on saving himself some maternity leave or pondering whether to promote you. If you are uncertain, you may choose to be diplomatic and find a way to say something consistent with the truth but not the whole truth: 'Well, who knows?' 'Sometime maybe?'

## SILENCE IS GOLDEN
## OR THE ANCIENT ART OF RESTRAINT

There are times when to tell the whole truth would in no way be helpful.

'How was my presentation?' asks the new employee.

'Probably the worst presentation I have ever seen in my life' is the sentence that may spring to mind but not quite find its way to the tip of your tongue. It may be the truth, but it won't necessarily help the employee to get better. This is truth that doesn't take account of either the person or the longer-term goal of training her to become a better presenter. Similarly, we can see in the way God acts towards us that he doesn't always reveal the whole truth about us all at once. He reveals what we can bear, what is genuinely helpful. When we are considering how much to disclose, our decision should be determined by love for the other person and by what is best for them, not by our fear of delivering uncomfortable news that may upset them. As the cliché tells us, sometimes we have to be cruel to be kind.

Conversely, there are times when we need to come clean and not massage the facts to save our own egos.

'Sorry I'm late. I was caught in traffic.'

Indeed I was, but the real reason was that I pfaffed around at the office and left twenty minutes later than I meant to. Anyway, the traffic is always bad at that time.

## HONESTY IS THE BEST POLICY?

Ashley works in sales for a major fashion label which sells into high-class stores. In front of him is a garment of which he has to shift thousands. In his opinion, it is not only highly priced and highly fashionable, it is also deeply ugly. He has sold none. One of the buyers arrives.

'Don't think much of that,' says the buyer.

'Ah, but the punters do. This is going to be really hot this season. Everyone's taking it.'

Let's run through that scenario again, but with one difference.

Ashley has recently committed his life to Christ. His sales techniques have helped him rise up the ladder, but they have also started to disturb him. In front of him is a garment of which he has to shift thousands. In his opinion, it is not only highly priced and highly fashionable, it is also deeply ugly. He has sold none. One of the buyers arrives.

'Don't think much of that,' says the buyer.

'No, me neither. It isn't selling well to other outlets, but it may do better in the smaller shops. It's got that offbeat ugliness that some people may actually like. But I wouldn't take many.'

The buyer doesn't buy many, but he finds Ashley's honesty refreshing. He now trusts him, and Ashley's sales figures continue to rise.

Truth builds trust.

Trust builds relationships.

Trust builds business.

In the end, people would rather do business with someone they can trust.

Honesty *is* the best policy, but sometimes it is very costly. People respect honesty but may sideline honest people.

Don was a senior manager in a bank. He was sidelined because he consistently made a nuisance of himself on issues of decency to customers and of fair working practices to staff. His warnings about the consequences of undue pressure and workload on staff went unheeded. One of his people committed suicide.

Don remained sidelined, his superiors embarrassed further by their failure to listen.

Fraser is an investment broker. He joined a major financial institution to sell an investment product that had been reported to have yielded returns well ahead of the market for years. Within three days he realised this wasn't true.

He questioned the numbers. Life started to become very difficult for him. He found himself a lawyer, documented every finding and eventually took the issue to the regulatory bodies. They agreed he had a case, but the City couldn't take another scandal. If he went ahead with it, he would probably be sued by the companies involved, tied up in the courts by heavy-duty lawyers, financially ruined and likely never to work again.

Fraser decided enough was enough. He negotiated himself out of his job, and joined another company for a salary and a position considerably less advantageous.

Sometimes the truth is very costly indeed. But, as one financial advisor put it in a seminar, not as costly as dishonouring God. And ultimately far more rewarding. Does he not promise, 'Those who honour me I will honour'?

Ultimately, our loyalty is to Christ.

## LATE

Like the white rabbit, Neil was late. Very, very late. For him. Five minutes late, to be exact. We were already looking around anxiously. Neil was the client, and Neil had a fifty-minute drive to get to our offices. But he was late.

Five minutes later and he still hadn't arrived. Someone was dispatched to phone his office. He had left over an hour ago.

We began to fear the worst. Neil was *never* late. Never once. Any other client, and we wouldn't have even been in the meeting room. We would be working away in our offices, wondering whether we had enough time to start and finish *War and Peace* before reception told us they had actually arrived. But if Neil said he would be there, he would be there. And he wasn't.

He arrived twenty minutes late, profusely apologetic. The traffic had been terrible. It never occurred to any of us that this was anything but the truth, the whole truth and nothing but the truth. Because it was Neil.

Reflecting on the sermon on the mount, Dietrich Bonhoeffer wrote: 'There is no need for an oath, because God is always listening, and the disciple always telling the truth. This must be their reputation.'

This was Neil's reputation.

And he wasn't a disciple.

# • 14 •

# WHEN THE HEAT IS ON

### or
### Business as usual?

*O Lord, who may abide in your tent?*
*Who may dwell on your holy hill?*
*Those who walk blamelessly,*
*and do what is right...*

Psalm 15:1–2, NRSV

Work is not morally neutral.

It is either conducted in a manner that is in line with God's word. Or it isn't. Every job has different kinds of ethical issues and every business is full of people making decisions about how to conduct that business. Here are six true case studies that may help you consider some of the issues involved in being a Christian in your workplace. The people involved faced quite different challenges and dealt with them as they thought best at the time. Were they right or wrong?

What would you have done?

• • •

# • CASE STUDY I •
## Should Carol sing?

Let's call her Carol, a 21-year-old trainee accountant, shy to the point of being deferential to supersoft teddy bears. She has been working in a small accountancy firm for about a year. One afternoon she is asked by her boss to put non-existent expenses onto a client's VAT return. This will mean that the client will pay less VAT than legally required.

At the same time Carol knows the firm are putting non-existent employees' salaries onto the client's payroll. Which means that the non-existent salaries can actually be paid to senior clients without those senior clients incurring a higher rate of income tax.

The senior partners in the firm are both Christians and knows what is going on.

What would you do?

### WHAT HAPPENED

Carol refused to do what her boss told her to do. He said, 'I could fire you.' She said, 'Fine.'

And he put the non-existent receipts on the VAT return himself.

This left Carol with another moral dilemma.

Should she report the manager to one of the partners, both of whom were Christians? Although they were aware of what was happening.

Should she confront them with their illegal and ungodly conduct?

Should she report the matter to the police or the Inland Revenue?

None of them easy options for someone who is deferential to supersoft teddy bears.

In fact, at the time, Carol didn't have the confidence to go to the authorities. She let the matter drop. She hoped that her own stand would speak to the manager and to her bosses. Five years on, with the confidence to take on a charging Siberian grizzly with a matchstick, she still believes it was the right thing to do at the time.

## • CASE STUDY 2 •
## The cost of honesty?

When Michael became a Christian, he had five girlfriends, two mortgages, a pile of debt and a thriving picture-framing business.

First to go were four of the girlfriends, leaving Lise, the Christian woman he had known for three weeks who had lead him to Christ. But he still had two mortgages and a pile of debt. He also discovered he had a nagging conscience, telling him he really ought to have registered for VAT and fully disclosed his income. He hadn't been registered for VAT or fully disclosed tax for seven years. It amounted to a lot of money. And would massively increase his debt.

Michael went to an accountant for advice. The accountant told him that the best thing to do would be to say nothing to the Inland Revenue and simply close down the current business and open up a new one in a new location. This way, all back tax and VAT would be neatly avoided. The Inland Revenue would never know. Sensible advice. But also illegal.

What would you do?

### WHAT HAPPENED

Michael decided to come clean. To register for VAT and fully disclose his prior income. It put him under immense pressure financially.

He also decided to register his employee for national insurance, even though the employee was happy to continue with the prior arrangement.

His friends tried to dissuade him. When he went to buy materials for his shop, he was encouraged by the salespeople not to pay the VAT.

'Nobody else does.'

'You're a mug, mate.'

Michael paid it.

On one occasion the shopkeeper simply pocketed the money himself and didn't register the purchase for VAT.

Michael's turnover, though healthy, wasn't high enough to service all his debt. He went bankrupt. And there was some risk that Lise, now his wife, might have to give up her course at Bible College. But somehow there has always been enough money – just.

Lise reacted this way: 'It's like that occasion in John's Gospel when a lot of people have left Jesus and he turns to Peter and says, "Are you leaving too?" Peter says, "Where shall we go? You have the words of eternal life." There's nothing else for us to do. You can live dishonestly as a Christian and have uncomfortable feelings, but you know you're going to be accountable for it in the long run.

'We know we've done the right thing, even though it's been like being squeezed through the eye of a needle.'

Michael is still in the picture-framing business.

His landlord has allowed him to stay rent-free until there is another tenant.

## • CASE STUDY 3 •
### A charge in question

Tom works for a major national building society. He is a branch manager.

He is told by his area manager to add on account charges to clients who have proved a nuisance. There is no legal or contractual basis for this increase. Tom objects, and is told that he can do it or leave: 'There are plenty of other people who would like your job'.

Subsequently, the area manager sets targets for all branch managers, of increased client charges of £10,000 per quarter per branch. £40,000 per year per branch.

The branch managers object at an area managers' meeting. They are told that this is a directive from headquarters. They can do it or leave.

Tom knows this is wrong. He registers his objection, but is again informed that he can do it or leave.

What would you do?

## WHAT HAPPENED

Tom realised that the building society was no longer the same place he had joined. Customer care was being sacrificed to short-term gains. The opportunity to develop real relationships with clients was being diminished by a policy of high personnel mobility. The industry-wide credit roll-over policy was not in the customers' interests, but rather a mechanism to get them deeper and deeper into debt and tied into the building society for the long-term.

He decided to be proactive and ask for voluntary redundancy when the next round of redundancies came up. His manager agreed. In the meantime, Tom was sidelined to a low-profile branch. He was given redundancy at the next opportunity.

Subsequently, he joined an estate agency. He resolved never to lie, and he informed his new employer that he would never do so. He intended to be in Bible College in a year's time, so he didn't care if they fired him. As he put it, 'I had nothing to lose'.

Tom soon gained a strong reputation for his truthfulness. On one occasion he negotiated a price of £80K for a new house. The client agreed. However, when Tom went back to the builder, the builder denied he had agreed that price and asked for £82K. Tom challenged him.

The builder continued to deny he had said £80K. Tom went to his superiors in the estate agency and told them about the problem. They called up the builder and said, 'We know Tom doesn't lie, so the price must have been £80K.'

Tom's reputation led his colleagues to support him.

## • CASE STUDY 4 •
## The thing about fish

The thing about fish is that if you take a ton or two out of a fish farm, you often can't tell that they are gone. It isn't like a nappy warehouse — if you take ten pallets of nappies from the warehouse shelves, there is a gap in the shelves. Take a ton of fish out of a tank, and there are still plenty of fish in there and still plenty of water.

Jimmy worked as the chief accountant in a fish-processing business. He noticed that they were receiving deliveries of fish, but were not always getting invoices for these deliveries. He told his boss, the managing director, that this was happening, and added that from now on he would send receipts of delivery to the suppliers who might never notice that the fish had gone.

His boss told him not to, arguing that this was business. If a supplier failed to invoice them, it wasn't Jimmy's responsibility.

What would you do?

### WHAT HAPPENED

Jimmy sent delivery receipts to the company's suppliers.

A while later, Jimmy's purchasing department faced a crisis. The management team were discussing their desperate need for a large delivery of fish the following day. They could find no one who would supply them.

Jimmy offered to help. They guffawed, saying, 'What can you do? You're just the accountant.'

He called the company he had been sending delivery receipts to. The fish were delivered the next day.

The team were amazed. His boss asked Jimmy how he had managed it. He told him.

His boss was furious and called him into the next board meeting, intending to gain board support for a formal reprimand.

But the board, much to the managing director's surprise, applauded Jimmy's actions.

## • CASE STUDY 5 •
## A low bid

Gerald is the bid manager for information systems in a major government department. The information systems unit has been subjected to a market test to compete for a £100 million account against a number of major companies.

In order to compete, they have formed a liaison with another major company. Failure to win the bid would almost certainly mean the closure of the unit, with the loss of up to 135 jobs. The policy adopted by Gerald's boss, the director of the unit, was 'We have got to say we can do everything, even though we can't'.

This meant saying that they could offer a standard of service they knew they couldn't deliver: an unattainable percentage of faults rectified within two hours, targets for delivery of goods they couldn't meet given the global chip shortage, and so on. In addition, the tender had been phrased to make it look as though the base-line service was higher than it was, giving the impression that fewer projects would have to be separately funded. This was a lie, though the wording was clever enough to allow for both interpretations.

Gerald objected to his superior. His objection was respected, but overruled. 'Conform or take redundancy,' he was told.

The team also considered industrial espionage using computer technologies to access rivals' bids. Again, Gerald objected.

Overall, he felt that his previous bid strategies – tough but honest – had worked, and he was aggrieved that the strategy had been changed. He also recognised that the data communications business was extremely cut-throat and it was more than likely that other contenders were also promising more than they could deliver. As another person in the industry put it, 'Everybody does it, because they know the accountants will simply choose the lowest bid. This may not always be the case, but it captures the context in which Gerald worked.

What would you do?

## WHAT HAPPENED

Gerald took voluntary redundancy. This came at a point when he had been feeling that God was calling him to theological college. He recognised that there were certain steps he could have taken. He could have blown the whistle to the National Audit Office. He could have written to the head of the civil service.

Both were high-risk strategies and would probably have resulted in the loss of the bid and hence the 135 jobs. Conversely, if the unit won the bid, the implication was that the tax-payer would pay the difference between the original bid and the real cost of the services required.

When he had gone to theological college, the unit offered Gerald consultation work. But once he discovered that the terms of the bid wouldn't be changed, he turned their offer down.

# • CASE STUDY 6 •
## To copy or not to copy?

Diane is a secretary in a London company. A friend of hers asks her to do a small amount of private photocopying for him. At first she accepts, but then she begins to have second thoughts. She knows there would be no point in paying for it – the accounts department wouldn't know what to do with such a small sum.

What would you do?

### WHAT HAPPENED

Diane decided that she would simply be taking advantage of the goodwill of her company if she photocopied the material, and she refused to do it. She returned the originals to her friend. He accused her of hypocrisy, saying she had never been so strict about such matters before. She replied, 'I've got to start somewhere.'

Big things, little things – we've all got to start somewhere.

• • •

# YOU'RE THE BOSS TOO?

*Question: What, apart from giving you a pay-rise every six months, are the characteristics of a good boss?*
*Answer: Ears.*

Roger Howe, maintenance officer

*O! It is excellent to have*
*a giant's strength,*
*but it is tyrannous to use it like a giant.*

William Shakespeare

## REVENGE IS SWEET

Recently my PA acquired a new toy. It is a doll about fifteen inches high. He has a corporate look about him – pinstriped trousers, and matching tie and braces. There's a whip in one hand and a Churchillian cigar in the other, and he's wearing a badge which says, 'Because I'm the BOSS'. He has a severe, somewhat maniacal look about his beady-eyed face and one of his employees is hanging by his trousers from his capacious jaws. Interestingly, his limbs and his head are attached to his body with Velcro. When you're stressed out with your real boss, you're supposed to rip this little fellow limb from limb and head from torso. And throw the pieces against a wall. Or maybe stamp on them.

I don't know why my PA has acquired this toy.

He has brown eyes like me. And dark hair like me. But he has no beard, and his nose is no rival to Concorde. Must be the other guy my PA works for.

The stereotypical image of the boss is of the one we love to hate – a paragon of unreason, impossible demands, contradictory instructions, bad jokes guffawed at with counterfeit glee. Still, an awful lot of us have people working for us. An awful lot of us are bosses. Are we like that?

I don't know if I'm a good boss. I do know that when I asked people in my workplace to quickly jot down a few words about the characteristics of a good boss, no one wrote back, 'Look in the mirror, sweet angel'.

I wonder what you think are the characteristics of a good boss. Here are some of the things my colleagues wrote:

- Listens to his staff. Is impartial between staff. Makes decisions that are considered, wise and reliable. Is able to do the hard things fairly and firmly.

- Knows where she wants the organisation to go, tells me, helps me to help her get there, and thanks me on arrival.

- Willing to listen, cooperative, decision-making, analytical, clear, resilient.

- Hardworking, trustful, thoughtful.

- Shows respect. Is interested in my personal welfare (other than to do with work), a good listener, takes my comments and suggestions seriously, gives feedback.

- Communicates, delegates, doesn't interfere in one's work or correct employees in front of others, has a sense of humour, treats one as an intelligent being.

- Sticks up for his employees. Leads by example. Is pastorally concerned, but wields a heavy hand when necessary. Asks the right person to do the right job.

- Lets you get on with your work, but doesn't mind if you come running when it all goes horribly wrong. Is patient, has a sense of humour. Much the same as a good husband really. Though he doesn't have to be at least six foot tall, have straight teeth and be able to sing in tune. (Applications, preferably with a photo to...)

- Encourages. Is occasionally appreciative, considerate, well-mannered. Delegates. Is completely open about the work and his expectations.

- Listens to ideas/points of view. Delegates responsibility. Allows a person to use his initiative. Is approachable. Is for a person's development.

- Cares about me and knows his job.

The business of leading and managing people has become a big business all of its own. Airport and station bookshops are full of books about it, intended to lure busy bosses (at least the ones who don't have laptop computers) into using their travel time to improve job performance, managerial skills, career progress and, of course, that most insistent of taskmasters – the bottom line. Gleaned advice from the Japanese, from what Harvard Business School doesn't teach, from dolphins and Attila the Hun, and from more benign leaders like John Harvey Jones and Lee Iacocca.

It's not my intention to evaluate the whole gamut of material on offer nor to look at how to improve particular management skills. Rather, I would like to focus on a small number of biblical principles.

If you look again at my colleagues' responses, you will see how they could be broken down into four main areas:

- **Vision and direction.** Someone who knows where they are going and what they want done, who knows the task and can set direction.

- **Competence.** Someone who can do his/her own job and can help me do mine.

- **Integrity.** Someone to look up to – a person of integrity, who is hardworking, trustworthy, honest, open, loyal, fair.

- **Love.** Someone who listens, respects, is concerned for his employees, has a sense of humour, can build a team.

Of these the last one – love – is perhaps the most startling and the one that you are unlikely to find in many management textbooks. Though, to be fair, you will find many of its manifestations – listening, developing, and so on. There is, however, a critical difference.

The Christian boss behaves in certain ways not because they will affect the bottom line but because those ways are consistent with what God has to say about dealing with people.

The Christian boss doesn't simply respect his employees because employees who feel respected work better, faster and more cost-effectively, but because the Bible says that people are infinitely valuable.

The Christian boss is concerned for his employees as people, rather than as cogs in the company machine. He is concerned for them not just because happy, healthy, stable people work better, faster, cheaper, but because people are always more than they do, more than the functions they perform at work.

The guiding principles for good management must, at root, be theological ideas, derived from God's character, Christ's example and the words of scripture.

## THE SERVANT BOSS

Three linked ideas seem to dominate what God is looking for in a leader. A clue to the first is in Solomon's prayer at the beginning of his reign:

> 'Now, O Lord my God, you have made your servant king in place of my father David. But I am only a little child and do not know how to carry out my duties. Your servant is here among the people you have chosen, a great people, too numerous to count or number. So give your servant a discerning heart to govern your people and to distinguish between right and wrong. For who is able to govern this great people of yours?'
>
> The Lord was pleased that Solomon had asked for this. So God said to him, 'Since you have asked for this and not for long life or wealth for yourself, nor have asked for the death of your enemies but for discernment in administering justice, I will do what you have asked. I will give you a wise and discerning heart, so that there will never have been anyone like you, nor will there ever be.'
>
> 1 Kings 3:7–12

God's pleasure doesn't stem from the fact that Solomon asks for wisdom in itself. It stems from the fact that he asks for wisdom for a particular purpose – so that he can govern God's people and do it justly. The wisdom he seeks isn't primarily for himself but for the people he is going to govern. His desire is selfless. And it is contrasted with a set of desires that would have been selfish – wealth for himself, long life for himself, security from his enemies. In contemporary terms – a fat annual bonus, a fabulous pension package and the demise of all serious competitors for his job and his company's customers. It is wisdom put at the service of others. The motive is love for God's people, as well as a keen sense of personal inadequacy for the task ahead.

God gives us gifts not just for ourselves but to serve others. The Christian boss, manager, leader is always a servant. Obviously he still exercises authority and power, just as Jesus did, but he does so with other people's interests at heart: 'Each of you should look not only to your own interests, but also to the interests of others' (Phil 2:4). How far do you have your people's interests at heart? Are you a servant leader?

Are you concerned about your people's development or only concerned about the extent to which they can contribute to your advancement?

Do you want them to grow as people as well as operators? Do you pray for wisdom and discernment in helping them develop? Are you honest with them about their prospects for advancement and rewards?

And how do you regard those in the company who do apparently less important work?

## UNCOMMON COURTESY

David Warden is a Christian ad executive. He left one agency to join another. His former president wanted him to come back. He was not only a first class ad executive but, she had come to realise, the most 'loved' man at his old agency. He made a huge difference to morale. In his new company, a secretary was introduced to him. She said, 'Oh, you're David Warden. You're the one who says "Hello" to receptionists. I've been dying to meet you.'

Simple, common courtesy. Treating people with

respect whatever their rank. And so rare in the corporate world as to be noteworthy. No wonder people love David. No wonder people love to work for David. He treats them with love.

God is love. But that doesn't make him soft, or ill-disciplined, or tolerant of slapdash mediocrity. Skills and standards are important, not just in themselves but for the impact they have. You don't love people by circulating poorly constructed, vague, over-full agendas. You don't love people by delegating work to them which they have neither the skills nor the resources to accomplish. You don't love people by putting off telling them that areas of their job performance are inadequate just because you will find the conversation uncomfortable. Firing them is a lot more uncomfortable.

## JUSTICE

The second criterion is justice. The good boss is a just judge. Rewarding people according to merit and effort. Promoting those with the skills for the job, not those who know how to ingratiate themselves with their superiors. Very few things are more corrosive in an organisation than the sense that politics or the application of emotional pressure will be rewarded more highly than merit. It rankles in every heart, and tends to make many people spend more time working out how to look great than working out how to do work that's great.

Justice also has a bearing on protection. Interestingly, the righteous king in Psalm 72 isn't evaluated by the way he treats his generals, high priests and chief administrators, but by the way he administers the law to those who have no power before the law:

> He will defend the afflicted among the people
>  and save the children of the needy;
> he will crush the oppressor.
>
> *Psalm 72:4*

Elsewhere, there is an emphasis on defending the alien, the widow, the orphan – people with no one to intercede for them.

The measure of a good leader isn't how she treats the people she needs – but how she treats the people who are less important and who have no apparent, direct bearing on her advancement. In God's field of vision the 'little people' loom large. How do you treat them?

## BRINGING OUT THE BEST

The third quality is genuine care for the people who work for you as people. The righteous king in the Old Testament is also the caring shepherd – providing, nurturing, protecting, developing. Again, this has nothing to do with being soft on poor performance or losing sight of the task to be accomplished, but everything to do with helping people do their best, give their best, be their best. And this is going to change from individual to individual. The good boss treats everyone fairly but doesn't treat everyone the same.

One of my bosses used to say to me, 'If you buy a dog, don't bark yourself.' I was the dog. It was my job to bark. He gave me clear overall direction, clear goals, but a lot of leash on how to reach them. Freedom for initiative. And a genuine sense of responsibility. It was just right for me at that time. At other stages of my career he might have responded differently. I would have needed a lot of supervision, a lot of teaching. The key to being a boss is being able to discern how to be there for people at the different stages of their development – offering help, or leaving the door open, or showing someone how to do something. This goes beyond simply recognising what advice and/or resources they need to get the job done well but extends to their personality needs.

Take, for example, a woman who has just finished some very important work that is going to be shown to a client the next day. She goes into her male boss and says joyfully, 'It's done. Would you like to see it before the meeting?' He trusts her and knows she is good at what she does. He is a 'new man' and doesn't want to patronise his female subordinate in any way. In fact, he wants to affirm her. So he says, 'No, thanks. I'll see it at the meeting. I'm sure it's great.' She leaves the room disappointed, thinking he doesn't really care. It wasn't the right way to handle her. And, though I'm now entering the minefield of gender differences here, research does suggest that it might not have been the right way to handle many women in that situation, although it might have been the right way to handle a lot of men. The point here is not to enter into a discussion of the different ways men and women communicate and prefer to be communicated with, but simply to make the crushingly obvious but vital point that we can never apply a simple formula to people. The good shepherd knows his sheep by name.

The good shepherd also helps his people to grow. This can sometimes mean encouraging them to look for different work or work elsewhere. Not so long ago I had someone reporting to me who worked hard, was smart and apparently competent but who didn't really produce the results. Week by week, I would try to show him how to do this particular job. Finally, I came to two conclusions. First, this person was in the wrong job and should leave. Second, I would in all honesty be able to give him an excellent reference for the right job. It was simply a case of being a square peg in a round hole.

I summoned up my courage to talk to him about it at our weekly update meeting. He walked into my office and, before I could say anything, told me he had come to the conclusion that the job simply wasn't him and he would like to leave. He hadn't been particularly happy, and he had the wisdom to see his situation clearly and to do something about it. But he might not have, and we don't do anyone any favours by leaving them in jobs that they don't do well and that don't really suit them.

The good shepherd looks after his people as people. Fights for better working conditions. Proper training. Fair rewards. And the right perspectives about the place of work in people's lives.

## LIFE BEFORE WORK?

A while back Tony had a heart attack.

It was his second.

He is a senior financial services salesman with a role in the office and a role on the road. A lot of pressure. He is married and has two children. His doctor told him to take it easy.

His manager, Gerry, is a Christian. He went to see Tony in hospital. He suggested that Tony take a disability pension or come back part-time. Less money, to be sure. But less pressure.

Tony wasn't too thrilled. He wanted his old job back. And, in a sense, he had a right to it. Gerry pointed out that maybe his family would rather live slightly less well and have him alive than have an empty place at table. Gerry asked other Christians to pray about it.

Tony appealed to Gerry's bosses. He won and found himself in a job just like his old one in a different branch of the company. He had a third heart attack. But he is still alive. Gerry did all he could to look after his employee's best interests, to put life before whatever it was that motivated Tony to risk it.

## THE BOSS'S SERVANT

Finally, Solomon has one more lesson for the Christian boss. Three times in his prayer he calls himself God's 'servant'. Solomon has a keen sense that he gets his authority from God. That God made him king. That it is God to whom he is ultimately accountable. Jesus, as we saw in chapter ten, makes the same point to Pilate – he would have no authority if God hadn't given it to him.

This is a radical perspective. God has given you authority, not ultimately your company. And ultimately you are accountable to him. Certainly, your workplace may well have particular criteria for evaluating people's performance and potential, and may have set aside certain funds for developing and training them. But are these in line with God's criteria and development programme? Do you need to supplement them in some way? Do you need to work to have some of them changed?

As God's servant, as your people's servant, what is in their interests?

## • SNAPSHOTS •

### Opportunity lost?

Let's call her Deborah. A wonderful person I'd been working with for over a year. She was Jewish, knew what I believed and had never raised the subject. Nor had I. It had never seemed right. We respected one another. I knew I could have talked to her. And I knew she would have listened. But I also felt that it would have been an abuse of our friendship. I would have been forcing something on her. So I never said anything overtly about the gospel. But I wanted her to hear it.

One day we were at a client's and due to travel back on the train together. I thought that there might be an opportunity to share something with Deborah. Towards the end of our meeting, our client said, 'Oh, are you travelling back by train? I'll come with you.'

'Aaagh! Nooooo! That's really blown it now,' I thought, but managed to feign delight. So we all toddled off to the train station together.

Five minutes into the train journey, completely out of the blue, with no preamble, no warning, no sidling cautiously up to the subject, the client, not a Christian, asked me why I believed what I believed.

So I told her. After all, she was the client.

And, of course, Deborah was sitting right there with us. So she heard the gospel too.

I didn't have to engineer anything. I didn't have to manipulate a situation in which I could talk at her about Jesus. I didn't have to steer the conversation round to a religious topic. I didn't have to do anything. God arranged it all.

### Fourth time lucky?

Jim had failed his professional exams three times. And he wasn't putting money on himself to pass fourth time round.

Tara was leaving the company but said to him, 'I'll pray for you.' She had developed the kind of relationship where she could say that kind of thing.

And she did pray.

Every day for a week until Jim's exams.

Four months later Tara went back to visit. Jim came running towards her like a long-lost lover in a romantic film. Or looking as romantic as you can look running round a corner, weaving between the photocopier and the rubbish bin.

'All those prayers worked,' he said. 'I passed.'

Others might be sceptical. Jim himself had no doubts. Even though he was an avowed atheist, he knew, in this instance at least, where the bottom line was. And he wasn't worried about the apparent contradiction.

## You never can tell

My boss had everything. A wonderful wife. Two lovely kids. Lots of friends. A great job with a great future, and the respect and affection of those he worked for and those who worked for him. He also had a beautiful house. With a golf course across the road, and a ten handicap. This was a man without any needs. Except perhaps a little more accuracy with his fairway woods. I'd been praying for him.

One day we were going on a field trip together. Two men on a plane. Two men in a car. Two men wandering around a lot of supermarkets looking at cans and jars of coffee on shelves. Lunch with two other people. Two men in a car. Two men wandering around more supermarkets looking at cans and jars of coffee on shelves. It's all glamour in advertising.

We talked a lot. Actually, I tell a lie. Probably *he* talked a lot. And there's only so long you can talk about cans and jars of coffee. So we talked about pretty much everything else. All day we talked. Or, probably, he talked.

I had prayed for an opportunity to talk about spiritual things. None came. Two men in a car. Then two men on a plane on a two-hour flight back. He talked.

We were almost there. Then the captain comes on: 'Due to heavy traffic into La Guardia tonight we'll be up here a while longer. So sit back and relax and, as soon as we know, we'll let you know when we'll be touching down.'

He carried on talking. We carried on circling New York.

I have to say I was getting a bit frustrated. There was absolutely no hint of an opening. I suppose I was altogether too focused on waiting for an opportunity to press my 'Here's the gospel' button rather than just enjoying the conversation and getting to know my boss better.

Anyway we circled. And he talked.

Half an hour passed. Then, as he came to the end of describing a particular area of his life, I said, 'Well, it sounds like you've got everything pretty neatly tied up then?'

'Well,' he said, 'it's just this religion business that's bothering me at the moment.'

I didn't say much to that. He just talked about it for a while.

You never can tell what's going on with people, can you?

# RESOURCES

## PUBLICATIONS

*Ethos* is a glossy bi-monthly Christian business magazine which runs a series of training conferences in association with London Bible College. Contact Kamal Bengougam at Ethos Communications Ltd, Gainsborough House, 15a High Street, Harpenden, Herts AL5 2RT; tel 01582 766764.

*Faith in Business* is a quarterly journal relating Christian faith to the business world. Contact Dr Ian Groves at 4 Broughton Rd, Ipswich, Suffolk IP1 3QR.

Stephen Green, *Serving God? Serving Mammon? Christians in the financial markets*, Marshall Pickering, 1996. Short, clear and helpful.

Richard Higginson, *Mind the Gap*, CPAS, 1997. A well-produced resource exploring the doctrine of work by looking at four themes – creation, fall, redemption and future hope. Case studies and examples of a wide range of jobs. Worth checking to see if it suits your needs.

Miroslav Volf, *Work in the Spirit: Towards a theology of work*, Oxford University Press, 1991. A fairly weighty and stimulating exploration.

## INTERNET

**The Workout Project** has developed a network of people and organisations, and is expanding it constantly. Discussion panels are already in operation. Contact Julian Doncaster at The Workout Project, 249 Alfreton Road, Sutton-in-Ashfield, Notts NG17 1JP; tel 0976 706307; email: workout@doncaster.org The Workout

Project website can be accessed at http://www.don-caster.org/workout/

## ORGANISATIONS

**The Christian Association of Business Executives** organises an annual lecture and was instrumental in setting up the Institute of Business Ethics. This offers practical advice to companies wishing to implement effective ethical policies. For details contact Stanley Kiaaer at 12 Palace Street, London SW1E 5JA.

**Christians at Work** has a very broad network of Christian workplace associations, and may well have details of an association in your industry or profession. Contact Mr Rod Badams at 148 Railway Terrace, Rugby, Warks CV21 3HN; tel 01788 579738.

**The Christians in Public Life Programme** aims to help all Christians actively involved in public life to engage, share and work together. It does this mainly through conferences and the circulation of resource papers. Contact Dr David Clark at CIPL, Westhill College, Selly Oak, Birmingham B29 6LL.

**The Industrial Mission Association** is a network of industrial chaplains and lay associates who visit workplaces, support marginalised people and make connections between faith and daily life. Contact Rev Robin Blount at Rivendell, School Lane, Folkestone, Kent CT18 8AY.

**The International Chamber of Christian Commerce** seeks to apply biblical principles to all aspects of business both in the UK and abroad. Contact Michael Fenton-Jones at 51 Peverells Wood Avenue, Chandler's Ford, Eastleigh, Hants SO5 2BS; tel 01703 251588.

**The Ridley Hall Foundation** is concerned to relate Christian faith to the world of business, and runs a programme of two-day seminars for small groups of Christian people from its base at Ridley Hall Theological College. Contact Dr Richard Higginson at Ridley Hall, Cambridge CB3 9HG; tel 01223 353040.

**The UCCF Business Studies Group** runs two weekend conferences a year, one for senior managers and one for middle managers. Contact Rev Simon Steer at Christian Impact, St Peter's Vere Street, London W1M 9HP; tel 0171 629 3615.

**The WorkNet Partnership** runs life-skill training seminars with a Christian underpinning for secular businesses, and also seeks to resource customised evangelistic events for Christians. Contact Rev Geoff Shattock at 56 Baldry Gardens, Streatham, London SW16 3DJ; tel 0181 679 0457.